# Rambling on Saint Martin

*A Witnessing*

Gérard M. Hunt

Order this book online at www.trafford.com
or email orders@trafford.com

Most Trafford titles are also available at major online book retailers.

Printed in the United States of America.

ISBN: 978-1-4269-0045-7 (sc)
ISBN: 978-1-4269-0046-4 (hc)
ISBN: 978-1-4269-0047-1 (e)

*Trafford rev. 11/14/2013*

 www.trafford.com

**North America & international**
toll-free: 1 888 232 4444 (USA & Canada)
fax: 812 355 4082

# Contents

To the Memory of my Mother, Josephine Fleming (1910 -1996), of my Father, Max S. Hunt (1906-1962) and of Amelia S. Duchene, aka Granny Cunda (1908- 1957)

*** 

À la mémoire de ma mère Joséphine Fleming (1910-1996), de mon père Max S. Hunt (1906-1962) et d'Amelia S. Duchene, aka Granny Cunda (1908-1957)

# Acknowledgments

I do not approve of what appears to be a new style that relegates acknowledgments to the very back of books. My gratitude shall remain front, foremost and hopefully comprehensive.

This book is a collection of disparate material written over a period of some twenty-plus years from the mid1980s to 2009. Some of these articles appeared in the long-defunct *The Chronicle*, others in the still-current *The Daily Herald*.

With the exception of a few letters and items appearing here for the first time, all of these "ramblings" are presented in the chronological order of their initial publication. I have corrected a number of misprints and made a few minor revisions for the sake of clarity.

The dedicatory inscription placed at the threshold of each article neither indicates nor suggests any endorsement of the views expressed in my text by the person or persons to whom the article is dedicated. These inscriptions are meant as expressions of my gratitude, friendship, solidarity, admiration or affection.

Throughout this book, Sint Maarten and/or St. Maarten designate the Dutch side of the island. Saint-Martin and/or St.- Martin (with a hyphen) refer to the French side.

When I wish to reference the island entity, as is the case most of the time, I use Saint Martin or St. Martin (without a hyphen). All of this might seem fastidious, but I believe it is of fundamental importance, and I suspect that the naming of our people and of the island they inhabit will be the subject of much debate in the future.

*Rambling on Saint Martin* has its true beginning in 1989, with my *Notes of a Native Son* for *The Chronicle*. They were written and published with the encouragement and assistance of Mrs. Mary J. Hellmund, a gracious lady and her gentleman of a spouse, Mr. Roger F. Snow. Without their support, I would never have written most of the earlier items assembled in this book. And with no beginning, there could be no middle and no end. I am forever grateful to Mary and to Roger.

Not in the least because of the above, and despite the still serious shortcomings of the press on both sides of the island, Saint Martin - the entire island - owes an ocean of gratitude to Mary Hellmund and to Roger Snow. This by reason of the singular role this industrious and enlightened couple has played in journalism on the island for roughly one quarter of a century.

In *Under the Sea Grape Tree*, and elsewhere, Senator Will Johnson of Saba credits the late Joseph H. Lake Sr. (1925-1976) with "establishing a lively free press in the Windward Islands." Indeed, not since José H. Lake Sr., his sons Joseph H. Lake, Jr. and Lasana Sekou, as well as Mr. Will Johnson himself, has so much been done for this lively free press in the Windward Islands.

While we are in the shade of Mr. Johnson's sea grape tree, I must thank the foremost historian of the Windward Islands, and their most eloquent spokesman, for his input into the making of my little book. Though I have not had the pleasure and honour of meeting him, Mr. Johnson has always been one of my lighthouses, one of my beacons on the hill.

I had envisaged publishing one book in which I planed to gather my *Ramblings on Saint Martin* and some notes on Guillaume Coppier, the 17<sup>th</sup> century French chronicler. Three years or so ago, my friend and mentor, Professor Theodore J. Lowi urged me to treat the topics separately. I could never thank him enough for his expert counsel on that matter among others and for the more than generous foreword he sent me for these *Ramblings*.

Mrs. Angèle (Daniel) Lowi, her sister Jacqueline, their brother, my friend Joseph Daniel and his wife, Janet have been steadfast in their encouragement. My warm thanks to all of them.

I thank Dean Sean Carrington at the University of the West Indies for allowing me to use his image of one of our old familiar ramblers - the coralita - on the cover of my book.

My friend and former colleague Martine Delsemme transcribed most of the earlier newspaper articles. She also read the French texts. Her brother, Jacques Delsemme helped me with all computer work including designing the cover and scanning the images. I am indebted to Martine and Jacky.

Ms. Helen D. Beck of "Sea Breeze Productions", Vancouver, B.C. assisted with the editing of most of the English text, and at Trafford Books, my Publishing Consultant, Ms. Angeles Devesa and my Author Support Representative, Ms. Jennifer Bradley provided me expert assistance. Thanks go to all three of them.

A number of my friends in Saint Martin helped to make this book a reality through their kindness, their interest in the project and their encouragement. I will refrain from naming anyone for fear that I may overlook someone.

Finally, I have no adequate words for my gratitude to my wife Mary Francine Aurandt without whom - none of this- nothing.

# Foreword

To
*Rambling on Saint Martin*
*A Witnessing*

Gérard M. Hunt is a man without a country, trying to piece together in essays, editorials and scholarship a country of his own from three quite separate nations: French Colonial by birth and upbringing; United States by military service and higher education; and Canada by profession in teaching and scholarship. The three have by no means come together in a single national unity. His homing tendency seems to be towards Saint Martin, but St. Martin is itself an amalgam – a clump of volcanic earth still divided, for no good reason, between two independent sovereigns thousands of miles away. He is not a split personality. He is a unitary citizen without an integrated polity.

For a goodly portion of his adult life Gérard has been trying to create that polity for himself, in which he can live not as a comfortable exile but as a responsible and effective participant. His ideal may be ancient Greece, where polity and democracy were invented. But there was actually no unitary Greek polity; Greece was a conglomeration of city-states sporadically at war with each other. Gérard's country, full of space and time, will ultimately reside in his mind. And he has lots of company in his research through such literary personalities as Guillaume Coppier and Saint-John Perse, who were also torn between a here and an (over) there and became – to use Gérard's favorite self-designation sort of –ramblers.

Coppier, the 17th century French voyager was a man driven by curiosity and by a desire to better his lot in life. Born in Lyon in1606, Coppier spent a good part of his life rambling through the Atlantic and the Antilles, on the edge of famine, illness and death, returning to the homeland and back to mortal danger –as an indentured servant, sailor-privateer-slaver, colonist, colonizer, tobacco planter and chronicler. His *History and Voyage to the West Indies* (1645) that contains the very first impressions of Saint Martin stirred emotions in Gérard that led him to spend, on and off, most of his adult life working toward some rehabilitation of the chronicler. There is no mention of Coppier in this *Witnessing*, but the reader of *Rambling on Saint Martin* must also visit Gérard's forthcoming *Desperate in Saint Martin - Notes on Guillaume Coppier.*

Alexis Leger was born in Guadeloupe in 1887, to a French West Indian family of some repute. His immediate family left the island to settle in southern France when the young Alexis (future Saint-John Perse,) was twelve years old. Leger's/Saint-John Perse's poetry brought him the 1960 Nobel Prize for literature, and

> though he never returned to the French Antilles where many of his relatives still resided, though some accused him of disowning his past and his people, ... almost all of his poems explicitly testify to the importance of his French-Caribbean origins ... (Hunt)

Both of these writers were, like Gérard, ramblers of a sort. Coppier the baroque traveler could not resist the call of the Caribbean, but he could not stay there permanently. Saint-John Perse never returned to Guadeloupe. He remained "a sort of nowhere man ... a kind of everywhere man ..." (ibid). As Alexis Leger he had a brilliant career as a French diplomat, but he wrote his illustrious poetry under his chosen *nom de plume*, Saint-John Perse. And in giving himself a name, "he chose words, nomadism, traveling, rambling over settling-in" (ibid.)

These two men were Hunt archetypes. They were not actual models after whom Gérard crafted himself. On reading Gérard's *ramblings*, it is obvious why he was drawn to them. Both were travelers; Guillaume Coppier more literally and more modestly than Saint-John Perse whose boundless imagination roamed the universe.

It is no wonder Gérard called his writing *Rambling* and himself *rambler*. These designations are by no means signs of modesty or self-denigration. According to Boswell, *The Rambler* was a title chosen by the great Samuel Johnson for his new periodical, to be comprised of essays on subjects of contemporary concern, every Tuesday and Friday. He kept *The Rambler* alive without interruption from March 20, 1750, "till Saturday the 17th of March, 1752, on which day it closed ..." Boswell actually provides a footnote: "This circumstance is worth notice, for Mrs. Johnson died on the 17th." (Boswell, 1904:136) Closer to us, Harold Bloom, the acclaimed American literary critic and writer informs us that "Johnson had a particular regard for his series of periodical essays *The Rambler*, which I strongly share ... *The*

*Rambler* is his crucial contribution to wisdom literature." (Bloom, 2004: 182) Indeed, *The Rambler* succeeded, with those articles Johnson himself referred to as essays. How appropriate. Essay, from Montaigne's French, "essayer": to try.

Many of Gérard's essays are grave and penetrating trials. Many are sentimental – catching up with childhood comrades, sharing grief over a lost friend or relative. Several of these discourses are critiques of the wayward tendencies of French efforts to govern Saint- Martin from Paris through Guadeloupe. The most serious and extensive of essays aim at encouraging a greater sense of historical awareness and of community solidarity among St. Martiners:

> A community that does not record and analyze events is a community whose days are numbered. To be without a history is to be outside of time, to have no existence, to have no being ... (Hunt)

*Rambling* turns out to be a most appropriate title for this book because history is a ramble through time. As Alice (of *Alice in Wonderland*) put it, "If you don't know where you're going, any road will get you there." History does not know where it is going. Some will disagree, arguing that every history has a purpose; a teleology. Nonsense! History can only tell us where we've been; and history is only memory, which fades as footprints on sand or snow. There is no living memory as such. Memory is a parasite; it lives off the few treasures that are available to us by stories - rambles

– about lives, actions, triumphs, tragedies, loves and hates – and only then, if we are fortunate enough to have preserved those moments by language. And for St. Martiners there are many languages: French, Dutch, English, Spanish, Creoles and snippets of the languages of the original indigenous people of the Caribbean. The various Creoles provide the words and the music. If we don't ramble in print, we leave all of those treasures to die.

Gérard's essays will, I hope, be a wake-up call to all who would still like to be St. Martiners – wherever they may be. I join the author with gratitude to *The Chronicle* and *The Daily Herald*. It took generosity and courage to publish so many of these essays, because many of them were not written for casual reading.

Theodore J. Lowi
Ithaca, N.Y.
November 4, 2008

# In Lieu of Introduction:

Vietnam (1965-1966)

For Roy T. Fields of Tupelo, Mississippi with whom I shared

a fox hole in Vietnam; for Carol J. Kontos who tutored me long ago at the University of Bridgeport in Connecticut; for Jack and Karen Leblanc who did not forget me and for Mary Francine Aurandt who never gives up on me.

What has Vietnam to do with my "Rambling on Saint Martin"? The answer is elementary: this rambler is a St. Martiner which makes his rambling intimately connected, inextricably linked to Saint Martin.

I was going to send these trials of mine to be printed with no other preface than the foreword my distinguished mentor and friend had sent me. I reasoned and still do that with such an unveiling, such generous and well assorted flowers at the entrance of my little book, there was no need for any further introduction.

And then on December 8, 2008, on my way for a walk, I tuned in (VPR) Vermont Public Radio and happened upon the final minutes of a program that featured three elderly guests who had written articles in a collection of memoirs of World War II.

I was too late for the interview of the first guest. One of the two remaining authors had served as a Captain in the US army and had seen combat in France during the Second World War. The other, a lady, had spent the war years at home in the US as a young mother and housewife.

There were a few minutes remaining in the program when the interviewer asked the Captain if there was an event that stood out in his recollection of his involvement in the war. A halting voice explained: "I saw some of our boys cutting off the fingers of dead German and American soldiers, cutting off the fingers to pocket their rings." The interviewer then asked the Captain how he had coped with such an experience. The Captain replied: "I tried to forget it. I did not talk about it."

As I walked along the disused canal at Pointe-des-Cascades in Vaudreuil-Soulanges, I tried in vain to silence the voice of the old veteran who had also explained that his war experience had made him cynical. It was cold, but the sun was strong. I felt the way I used to in the Sandy Ground of my youth, when I awoke, almost every day, to a morning full of sunshine. I felt I could move mountains.

When I got back from the hour long walk, my face numbed by the minus fifteen December breeze, the afternoon was still as bright as it is almost every day of the year in Saint Martin. By the time I had warmed up in my car, stopped off to do some grocery shopping, and returned home, the sun was ebbing and my enthusiasm had long since receded.

As the snow-filled December days went by, I kept returning in mind to the interview. The brief exchange was reconnecting me with my past, with Vietnam, with my feelings of and on that period of my life; rekindling cinders still not completely reduced to ashes. But, at every step, this reawakening was meeting a well-anchored resistance: "Why revisit old wounds? Who cares anyway?"

I had returned from Vietnam, in 1966, to a nation where veterans, such as I, would soon be viewed as outcasts, pariahs of the worst order: depraved killers of women and children. Like that veteran of an earlier war, but for my own reasons, I tried to forget the past. I tried not to speak of Vietnam, of my experience of the war, of my feelings.

To this very day I have read nothing on the Vietnam War, not even the classic: *We were Soldiers once ...and Young*. I also stayed away from all films on the subject, even the one inspired by the account of that officer of our Division, Lt. Gen. H. G. Moore and the journalist J. L. Galloway. I did purchase a 2002 Harper Torch paperback edition of the book which I skimmed, but I have yet to read it. As for the various comedies and/or satires based on the war, I have often wondered if there are combat-veterans who could feel entertained by watching Robert Altman's "MASH" or any similar program. I had drawn a solid red line on all that was related to the Vietnam War.

It was, most definitely, my mentor's suggestion that I

touch upon my Vietnam experience in a preface to my book, his reference to my "military service" in the foreword he had sent me, along with the Captain's brief account of his war experiences that caused me to revisit that most difficult period of my life. And all of that led to this modest attempt at dealing with Vietnam and its aftermath.

I enlisted in the US Army in 1963. After basic training and airborne school, I was assigned to the 1st Battalion (Airborne) 187th Infantry, part of the 11th Air Assault Division (Test) at Fort Benning, Georgia. I served in Vietnam in the 1st Brigade (Airborne) of the 1st Cavalry Division (Airmobile); the "All The Way Brigade". I was a "grunt" and a "Charger" in Bravo Company, 1st BN 12th Cavalry (ABN).

Elements of our Division engaged the Vietcong and regiments of the Regular (North) Vietnamese Army on several occasions. We suffered a number of casualties and fatalities, but to my knowledge, we were never defeated in battle, not even in November 1965 when the enemy overran one of our battalions and so many of our buddies fell in the "Valley of Death."

We never failed to accomplish our mission. We always prevailed. They were the enemy. I was a soldier. I did what I felt I had to do. I presumed, and I still do, that the enemy soldier was in the same predicament as I. I have never lost any sleep over that aspect of my involvement in the war. And thank heaven I never witnessed any such atrocity, any such inhumanity as that described by that old World War II veteran.

What stands-out most in my memory of Vietnam are events of another order, or rather a number of occurrences that were significant to me and became etched forever in my mind's eye.

In1965, in June or July, not long before we shipped out to Vietnam on board of the USNS Geiger, I was told to report to my Company Commander. This, in itself, was quite unusual and I wondered why I had been summoned. I knew I had done nothing wrong and so I became convinced that something awful had happened back home in Saint Martin.

I felt an enormous relief when Captain Roll explained that as an alien enlistee I could decline to serve in combat, in which case I would be transferred to some other unit in the US, in Europe or elsewhere. I recall telling my CO that I wished to remain with my buddies with whom I had done all my training and that I felt I was well trained and ready for combat.

The first time I came under live fire in Vietnam, and felt, for a moment, that every incoming bullet was headed straight for the center of my forehead, I recall wondering if I had done the right thing that day in Captain Roll's office.

Not long after we arrived in Vietnam, Captain Roll was promoted to the rank of Major and, if I'm not mistaken, he was assigned to Reconnaissance, or to Intelligence. Later on, towards the end of my service in Vietnam, I believe he remembered me and was instrumental in sending for me when there was a need for someone to do some interpreting from French into English and vice versa. I was plucked from the jungle area where my unit was on combat operation and flown to Dalat in the center of what was then South Vietnam.

The month or so I spent in Dalat thanks, I believe, to my former Company Commander, was both a blessing and a burden. It was a blessing for it took me away from extremely hazardous duty during that period, and it was a psychological burden of sort in that I had to return to said duty when my assignment in Dalat ended. And returning was that more challenging given that I was "short," with not much time remaining before being eligible for discharge from the service.

I think this brief assignment in Dalat as an interpreter later inspired me to continue my education after I was discharged from the army and to choose teaching as a profession. Such is life, I believe; a web of chance encounters, of occurrences and events.

There was a night we moved through the jungle on a mission. As I recall, our Company was the lead company of the battalion, our platoon was the lead platoon of the company, our squad the lead squad of our platoon and I was point man in our squad during some forty or so eternal, agonizing minutes.

Drenched in sweat, bleeding from cuts inflicted by elephant grass, and plagued by leaches, every hesitant step in that pitch dark night was an ordeal; a step into a bottomless pit. Every minute of that point duty was an excruciating leap of faith given the knowledge that one of the most efficient and insidious weapons of the enemy was a spiked trap hole often as wide and deep as our widest, deepest fox hole. I don't recall the object of that mission, but I'm sure we had been briefed, at least to some degree, on the surprise that was intended.

By dawn, we had emerged from the jungle not far from a Montagnard village. Just before the sun started to pierce the horizon, their drumming began. It seemed progressive; a crescendo that appeared to mimic the gradual increase of sunlight and it climaxed when the sun finally cleared the horizon. Hundreds of loin-clad brown bodies were worshipping the sun, celebrating a new day. I remember thinking: "How wild and backward! How primitive and idolatrous!"

Thirty odd years later, the great ice storm of 1998 plunged vast areas of southern Quebec into darkness. A week or more went by without any sunlight whatsoever. One morning, standing on a porch in Sainte-Anne-de-Bellevue, as the first rays of the sun finally began to exit from behind the clouds of a still overcast sky, I was suddenly propelled back in time to that sunrise in Vietnam, but this time, the drumming was delightfully uplifting, for I had long since transcended the arrogant ignorance of my youth; I had long since connected with the wisdom and the ritual of the Montagnard.

And there was that day, another day in the jungle. A few of us had discerned faint noises coming from a cave on the bank of a river, and after shouting "Di di mau!" ("Hurry out!" in Vietnamese) several times, we were about to lob some grenades into the cave when there appeared a man, then another and a couple of women and children. They came forward and stood motionless at the entrance of the cave, not far from us.

Some of them had stumps in lieu of limbs, and they were, all of them, utterly, hideously disfigured. I immediately recognized them as lepers, but the astonished and horrified looks on the faces of my buddies led me to conclude that, unlike me, they had never seen a leper. We stood there a while, an eternity, staring at the poor devils stare back at us while our leaders decided how to proceed. Word finally came down and we turned in part of our rations, some of which we opened and left for them.

The event that stands out among all others in my recollection of my involvement in the war is not that night on point duty in the jungle, nor the sunrise ritual of the "Mountain People." It has nothing to do with the horrors of war; with witnessing comrades suffer horrible wounds, sometimes close to death. It has nothing to do with being targeted while moving through rice paddies where cover is limited and returning fire is difficult at best; with being pinned down by well camouflaged snipers hell bent on hitting their targets. It has absolutely nothing to do with chills brought on by malaria, or with a number of other singular occurrences, not even those ceremonial taps over the spit-shined boots of fallen comrades.

The most persistent and painful recollection of my involvement in the War is the image etched in my mind's eye of those desperate lepers we left standing at the entrance of that cave. Later, somehow, this picture, the scene of those unfortunate outcasts, expelled from their community, became fused with my self-victimization. I forged, and for the longest of time, I nurtured an obscene debilitating equivalence between the hopeless, utterly wretched condition of those desperate lepers and my relatively privileged plight as an ostracized Vietnam veteran.

I don't know what became of my former CO. As for my buddy Roy, who hailed from the same town as Elvis, I recall him once saying to me, as we sat on guard in our fox hole: "When I get back home, the first person that tells me I cannot enter a night club or sit where I choose on a bus, I'll ask them: And where the hell were you when the shit hit the fan in the Nam?" How could one forget such powerful pertinent poetry? I deeply regret not trying to locate Roy much earlier, not trying to keep in touch with him after I was discharged from the army and during all these years. I have searched for him and for our former CO in vain via the Internet. If still in life, I wish them both the best of health.

I've never been to Washington where the granite wall stands weeping from so many scores in its polished finish. Why they, not I? Was it faith, destiny, luck, chance, fortune, Divine providence? We are not worthy of the sacrifice, but we remember them. "They shall grow not old as we that are left grow old."

Indeed, they have not grown old, as we who were left grew old: Age has not wearied them, nor have the years condemned them. At the going down of the sun and in the morning, we remember them. (With Apologies to L. Binyon)

I've been a resentful Vietnam veteran for the longest of time. I know now that resentment is far worst than some permanent indigestion that sickens the body and consumes it rapidly as Nietzsche claimed. I think resentment is more like an insidious slow cancer that gnaws away at the root of one's being. I've been a resentful Vietnam veteran much too long.

In the cruel month of November when mums weep the morning dew, some day soon, I hope to be in Washington to stand a while beside the granite wall.

Gérard M. Hunt
Notre-Dame-de-l'Île-Perrot, Québec
January 6, 2009

"Our thoughts are the epochs of our lives; all else is but a journal of the winds that blew while we were here."

Henry David Thoreau

1850

# My Poetics: Rambling

Life is so short. The gap, or rather the awful chasm that separates mortal time from cosmic time, the time of the universe, is so overwhelmingly unbridgeable. Story-telling, narration, writing, may be one of the few viable temporary antidotes to the crisis most of us experience confronted with the silence, the indifference, the fathomless inscrutability of this chasm. Indeed, time may be nothing more than the narrative path we are traveling. Narratives help me cope with time. Every story I tell informs on who I am. *Rambling on Saint Martin* is my way of trying to make sense of time, my attempt at bridging the abysmal chasm.

« On aura compris que le temps est, en fait, la seule réalité vraiment rare: nul ne peut en produire; nul ne peut vendre celui dont il dispose; personne ne sait l'accumuler ».

Jacques Attali: *Une brève histoire de l'avenir* (2006)

"We will have understood that time is, in fact, the only reality truly rare: no one can produce time; no one can sell the time they have; no one knows how to hoard it."

Trans.: G.M.Hunt

# A Rambling Witnessing

To the Memory of my brother Raymond and my sisters Christiane and Rosita. For my sister Edmée

"Walking or wandering aimlessly; strolling or roving; following an irregular winding course of motion or growth; speaking or writing at length and with many digressions; roaming, roving, wandering." That's how most dictionaries define "rambling."

When I try to get a better grasp of the thing while still focusing on the word, a tune comes my way —I hear the sweet mellow voice of Nat King Cole singing "Ramblin' Rose."

In Cole's song, (words and music by Joe and Noel Sherman, respectively,) rambling is a secretive, somewhat unpredictable, undisciplined activity: "Wild and wind-blown," the rose rambles. To what end? No one knows. In Cole's song, there is no explicit reference to thorns, but everyone knows that the rambling rose is beautiful, but its stem or vine is full of prickles. Such a rambler may be loved with a "love true," but this love is almost never long-lasting, for who can cling at length to such a prickly thing?

"Who will love you with a love true when your rambling days are gone?" The answer to this rhetorical question is, of course, no one. No one will love this rambler when its roving days are gone. The fate of this rose is indeed a tragic affair, for if it cannot experience lasting love while it rambles, and if no one will love it "with a love true" when its roving days are over, what is left for this rambler to do?

Given the imbroglio, seemingly the most logical way out is that the rose foregoes its rambling that it abstains from all such activity. Another apparent reasonable alternative may be that it stops its roving before the onset of its decrepitude. Only then, could it be loved with a "true love."

But, of course, such options will not do, for they run counter to the very essence of a rover. Indeed, can one truly expect a born rambler to cease rambling? Is it not the nature of such prickly flowering shrubs to wander, to ramble on and on until they wither and die? Is that why Cole keeps telling the rose to ramble on?

You, my hurried reader, may still be wondering what this is all about. I would like to furnish you with *the* answer to my roving, the one that would put an end to your curiosity. Alas! It seems that with rambling it is as with life itself; there is no set answer. Every answer elicits yet another set of questions that postpones closure—the solid rock, the anchor some of us seek so obsessively.

Still, we strive to live our life. We carry on. We make believe we have found *the* answer, that we have finished the job. We pretend we have solved the problem and that we are moving on. In doing so, we are most likely yielding to the universe within us; repeating, turning, troping, putting in time until that day, that evening, that late afternoon or early morning we are spun off or swept into the vortex.

In either case, we are sure to miss the measured path by moving too close to the whirling center, or by wandering too far away from it, towards the edge where the turbulence is equally fatal.

Until then, my impatient reader, my soul mate, my friend, as in Cole's song, I'll just ramble on.

Author (On the left) and J. Daniel at Princess Juliana Airport (1961-1962)

# Do They See the *Foufou*?

(*The Chronicle*, November 8, 1989)

For James Chance, Roger and Michel Augusty, Oger Tondu and Joseph Daniel

Five o'clock in the afternoon, I sit quietly on the balcony. Nearby, on a wall, a lizard swells its neck and spreads a yellow fan. Suddenly I am back with Oger, James, Roger, Michel and Joe. I am back with the boys from the sand, the boys from Sandy Ground. Lizard fights! Like game-cocks, the lizards pounce on one another, they wrestle and bite. We laugh and shout as we pull them apart. The "grass lassos" are amazingly strong. The lizards sway inert in mid-air like corpses after the hanging in an old western film.

You, my reader, you do not understand what this piece is all about, and I do not either, but I had a little too much wine, and sometimes when this happens or when I get the blues, no matter where I am, like a homing bird, I fly back in thoughts to Sandy Ground with the boys from the sand. Of course, they might be surprised to hear this. I have never told them how I feel.

Do boys in Sandy Ground still fight lizards? Do they still put small smooth stones in slingshots to slay sweet little birds? Will they be spared the curse for having silenced a "Yellow Breast?" Will they suffer recurrent nightmares for having slain a humming bird? Will they, like me, see the "foufou" in their dreams?

Oger and James are still in Sandy Ground, the new Sandy Ground; the one that begins after the bridge. Oger has lost his wife after a long illness and, to date, has elected to bring up his boys on his own. Roger is in Staten Island. James has put away his dad's banjo, but he has taken up the horn. He sings and plays like Louis Armstrong. Michel drives his taxi and lives on the Dutch side with his wife and children. Joe is a P.E. teacher in Lansing, Michigan.

As for me, after a long time spent abroad, I am back at home to try to work, and to live and share my rambling thoughts with you in *The Chronicle* from time to time.

*\*foufou* : Local name for the hummingbird - Most likely a corruption of the French "froufrou" (rustle or rustling): an onomatopoeia.

# Hospitals and Funerals

(*The Chronicle*, November 15, 1989)

To the Memories of: Dr. H. Petit and Dr. G. Dormoy.
For Dr. F. Anaïs, Dr. Y. De polo, Dr. V. Gibbs, Dr. L. Jeffry,
Dr. F. Petit, Dr. M. Petit, Dr. G. Vialenc. For the nurses
and other health care givers in Saint Martin.

With all the talk concerning Port de Plaisance, Bellevue,
the frontier and its monument, I had decided to voice my
opinion on the matter, an opinion based upon information
I had managed to gather. It is so difficult to speak
intelligently about anything. One must always wonder if
one has enough information on the subject, whether or
not one's sources are reliable, if one's grasp of the context
is adequate, whether or not one's tone is appropriate. I had
already jotted down the main points I would develop, but
late that afternoon, I went to the hospital in Marigot to
visit two old friends, and somehow, Bellevue, the frontier,
and its monument slipped into the background.

When I arrived at the hospital, I learned that a relative
of mine was also there and very ill. There is something about
hospitals that gets to the core of my being, something that
goes straight to its center and shakes the very foundation of
it all. No, it's not only the fact that I'm afraid of becoming
ill, very ill, that I'm afraid of suffering, and thereby causing
those who love me to suffer with me. No, it's more than all
of that. It's a feeling that comes over me and speaks to me,

and even though I understand its message, I'm very much at a loss for words to describe it.

Maybe that's why I'm so in awe of those who spend their lives in or around hospitals, caring for the sick: doctors, nurses, all hospital workers. Yes! Hospitals and funerals get to me. They jolt me back to the essentials of existence, to the question of life and death, or should I say to the question of life-death.

If I were a judge, I would use hospitals and funerals as agents, as instruments of rehabilitation. I would require criminals to visit hospitals and to attend funerals. The sick, the dying, and the dead might speak softer, deeper, fuller and further to the disorder in the mind, in the psyche of a criminal.

I entered the hospital room. Fred greeted me with a smile. A smile tells me a lot about a person, or rather, for me, a person is like their smile. Fred's smile is gentle, soft; a sweet and soothing smile that says: "You're OK. You can talk to me; I'm listening, really listening."

Almost any one of the boys will tell you that there is a void in Marigot since Fred Trene has had to leave his shop. We had a long chat, and then Fred began to talk to me about the man in a bed on the other side of the room. He must have noticed me glancing at this man, who had several books open on his bed and seemed immersed in his reading, oblivious of the world. Lowering his voice, Fred explained: "A doctor! A bright man, a good man... He used to come by me a lot...We used to talk a lot...A real brainser!* But he fall apart when his wife leave him. He say she take all the money and disappear, but who really know why she do him that? Look at him! All day, all night in his books, reading, reading…" And I looked at the man crouched over the books, but I couldn't help saying to myself: "There is my Freddie, praising, never blaming, never denigrating, always praising…"

After my visit with Fred, I went to see Vital. He was on his back, his right arm tied gently to the bedstead. (A nurse explained that he was scratching and hurting himself.) His right leg, from the knee down, was hanging over a metal retainer at the side of the bed. He kept swinging this leg back and forth.

As I stood there looking while a loved one fed him like a child, I kept wondering if this swinging of the right leg was his way of telling me that he was aware of my presence, his way of inducing me to concentrate, to focus on his right leg, the one that was so quick. That was the leg we feared so much when he played against us "Golden Stars," the one he used to beat time, and to move with rhythm as he stood playing the lead pan next to Pétain. Vital, the music man, the master football player…Yes! That's the same leg, and it kept swinging.

After she finished feeding him, she held him up with her right arm and made him drink his medicine. The leg kept on swinging, swinging…then she wiped his face, and while stroking his head, she leaned over, and with her lips almost touching his left ear, she began to whisper a prayer:

"Our Father who art in heaven…" and the swinging grew slower, slower, slower, then it stopped.

The door to Harry's room was closed. I stood in front of it wondering what to do. An elderly lady approached me. I didn't recognize Harry's mother. I told her who I was. She greeted me warmly, inquired about my mother, and led me in to her son. Harry seemed pleased to see me. He kept asking about my sisters and my mother. He was anxious to see his daughter, the one arriving from Holland on Air France. She was due at the hospital any minute. Harry's eighty-year-old mother, frail but alert, was seated in front of me. She had spent several evenings there with her son. We talked. Harry kept correcting her: "No, that's his other sister. You don't remember her?" Then Harry's daughter arrived and his face lit up. It was time for me to let them be alone.

As I walked down the corridor of the hospital and out to my car, I kept wondering how awful it must be for a mother to see her child very ill, near death, or in death, and my thoughts went back to my mother in Canada, and to my brother Raymond who died last year.

*St. Martin slang word: A very educated and/or very intelligent person.

# Salt and Sun

*(The Chronicle,* November 22, 1989)

For all my former colleagues at the *Lycée des Iles du Nord* and at the *Collège du Mont des Accords*

Any good English dictionary will inform us that the word "frontier" comes from the Latin "frontis" meaning "the leading edge of the body," the forehead. Of course, the forehead will only be the leading edge of the body if or when one assumes certain postures, certain stances. At rest, the leading edge of the body for most of us nowadays is the stomach. The leading edge of the Roman foot soldier, the one that did most of the fighting, was his forehead. The word "frontier" most likely refers back to those days when men, weapon in hand, defended what stood behind a line they had drawn, a trench they had dug, a wall they had built, a flag they had planted. So much for the word, now what about the thing?

The frontier that runs East-West or West-East, scarring the map and the land, dividing the island into "Northern Saint-Martin" and "Southern Sint Maarten," is a very real line. It is physical and legal. It is true that persons and goods can circulate freely across it, but the fact remains that this frontier is a partition dividing the island into a French side, where the official language is French, and a Dutch side, where the official language is Dutch. To believe that there is one Saint Martin because there is "one people" is to act like the big bird that buries its head in the sand.

Now, what are monuments? What does the monument at the frontier represent? What does it make present now that was present once? What does it "re-present?" What does it bring back into our memory? What does it commemorate? Some argue that it brings back, it represents the agreement reached in 1648 whereby the island was partitioned. For them this monument is the constant painful reminder of a partitioning they view as a major obstacle to a further and fuller development of the "one people" of this Land. Others I have heard speaking out on this issue feel that the monument represents 341 years of peaceful co-existence and cooperation between French Saint Martin and Dutch Sint Maarten. I view this latter assessment as historically incorrect and profoundly disturbing. These fellow St. Martiners and others, confuse the people of this island with the past governments of Saint Martin and Sint Maarten.

Before 1848 (for the French side) and 1863 (for the Dutch side), the people of this island were in bondage. It is only in 1882 that the mayor begins to be elected by the people. Up until then, he is appointed by the governor to neutralize and/or control the municipal council that is elected.

On the Dutch side, it is only in 1948 that the people are allowed self-government with the introduction of universal suffrage. Notwithstanding all of the above, because of a number of reasons too subtle to elaborate upon here, one might argue that there is still no true representation, no true local government.

As for the 341 years of friendship and peace between the French and the Dutch, in his "History of Sint Maarten and Saint Martin" J. Hartog informs us that the 1648 treaty was violated repeatedly, and sometimes completely forgotten. Indeed, the struggle for ownership and/or control of this island through invasion and occupation was mainly a European affair. The people of this island played a negligible part in this struggle. This struggle is clearly visible up until 1816, when the English returned the island to the French-Dutch governments. This battle is not over yet, but instead of fighting one another, the Europeans, the French particularly, but not solely, are pooling their investments, instead of harvesting salt, they are selling sun.

The frontiers of the world are not disappearing, as so many seem to think, they are merely moving, shifting. The Europeans are forming their economic block to better compete against the Asian block and the North American block. Who is looking after our interest? Who is insuring that we, who are neither European nor American, are not boxed in, that we are not squeezed to death by these blocks? Who is speaking for the St Martiner?

Now is not the time for St Martiners to sit and cry over the injustices of the past. Now is no time for personal attacks and petty recrimination. It is time for calm, collective, constant and careful dialogue aimed at promoting and enhancing the well-being of St Martiners. They kept us off all the old gravy trains: the salt train, and the tobacco train, and the sugar cane train. Now a new train has pulled into the station: the triple S train, the Sea-Sand-Sun train. We must, not only climb aboard this new train, we must be amongst its conductors, its engineers. We must demand to ride first-class on this new train.

# Language – Being

This piece appeared in *The Chronicle* on November 30, 1989, under a different title

For all my former colleagues at Milton Peters College

When I was a boy in Sandy Ground, the old Sandy Ground, one of the few obligations I had to meet was that of going to church on Sunday. I looked forward to going to Sunday Mass.

On Sunday, people were different; they looked different, smelled different. I liked attending "Sunday Mass," even though I could not understand what went on during the service, for it was said in Latin. I understood nothing, but I liked dressing-up and seeing people all dressed-up. I liked the scent of incense burning, and, at night, the flickering flames of the candles. Yes, I liked going to church, but oh, how I wished I were Methodist like my friend Oger and his grandmother "Tante" Mildred.

One Sunday, instead of going to church, I went and sat in a pew at the back of the Methodist chapel. I still don't know why we call one a church and the other a chapel. When I got home after the service, someone had already told my mother that I had gone to the chapel instead of the church.

My mother was waiting. She asked me how mass was. I

told her how nice it had been, except that the priest seemed annoyed by the crying of a little boy whose mother was not present. My mother got angry, but when I explained why I had done this awful thing, and inventing a story, she cooled off and I got away without a beating.

I recall telling her how much I liked the hymns, how I understood the prayers, how I enjoyed the singing of the congregation, how I understood everything Pastor Gibbs had preached in his sermon. Of course, I did not understand everything, but the sermon was in English and I could follow a bit.

This little anecdote is meant as an introduction to the subject I should like to ramble on about this time, namely language, and specifically, the language of instruction in the public schools of this island.

The debate concerning the language of instruction is a most important, most fundamental debate. It is intrinsically political. Everything is political, but there is nothing more political than language, for it is language that enables us to live in society. The words "politics" and "political" come from the Greek word "polis": "Having to do with life in the polis, in the community, in the city."

How could there be a society without language? Is not language the cement that binds individuals into families, towns, cities, nations?

Language is the vehicle in which everything must travel, but we cannot "get out" of language the way we get out of a car. No, the medium is truly, in part, the message. The great thinkers of all nations have underscored the importance of language. They have emphasized the very special relationship that exists between language and "being."

For the German philologist and philosopher Heidegger, "language is the shepherd of being." I like his metaphor, the mental picture, this short sentence evokes: language, there, like a shepherd looking over, protecting, one's being. One's language as the guardian of one's inner being. Indeed, disorderly language or speech is one of the first signs of ill-being.

Jean Piaget, Frantz Fanon and others have studied the language-being connection from a psychological and sociological standpoint. They have stressed the importance of language in the development of the personalities of children. The studies of Frantz Fanon, who was from Martinique and, to some extent, some of the writings of the novelist V.S. Naipaul, who is from Trinidad, should be required reading for all educators, including school administrators.

There is no doubt in my mind that students learn better and quicker when they get their instruction in the language they speak at home. I know that the vast majority of the people of this island do not speak the same English spoken in Great Britain, in the USA or in Canada. Given our history, this is quite normal, but our English is close enough to Standard English and our students would benefit tremendously from an educational system where the language of instruction is Standard English.

However, as we have already noted, language is inherently political, which means that any such change in the public educational systems cannot take place without concomitant changes in the political status. Politics and economy go hand-in-hand; therefore, our economy will be affected. How can we (French and Dutch Antilleans) attain fuller political unification with English, the language of the people, as the official language and the language of instruction in the public schools?

How can this be done while maintaining our specificity, our cosmopolitanism? Let us not fool ourselves. This is no little obstacle, for this specificity, this cosmopolitanism, fuels the economy of our homeland. If English is made the official language and the language of instruction in all public schools, would this island lose the specificity the old song refers to? Would we cease being "People French and Dutch, though talking English much" and become just another Anglophone island in the Caribbean?

Is political unification of this island possible at this time? Would the economic fallout be so noxious, so crippling, that it is sheer folly to entertain such a proposition? These are some fundamental questions I believe we must try to answer through reflection, discussion, dialogue and civilized debate.

Author's Most Cherished Diplomas
(His signature was added recently)

# It's not too late!

*The Chronicle*, December 6, 1989)

For Mary J. Hellmund and Roger Snow who encouraged me to write articles for *The Chronicle* and *The Daily Herald*

On Friday evenings, I try to relax and spend some time with friends. This is my way of celebrating that I have made it through the week, my way of coping, of getting prepared mentally, psychologically for the week ahead. On Friday nights, we have our little "punch avec sirop," and we set about solving the problems of planet Earth before tackling those of this island. After this brainstorming, I usually go home and sleep like a log except when I overdo the "liming." When I drink too much punch, I have bad dreams, veritable nightmares!

Last Friday evening, I met some friends. We solved all of Gorbachev's problems then we tackled crime and violence on this island. We didn't make much headway there. I had some punch, a little too much, I think. I went home expecting a nightmare. No such luck, not even a dream! I was disappointed when I awoke Saturday morning. I began to wonder what kind of nightmare I would have chosen Friday night if I could have ordered one the way we order a pizza.

I soon had the answer: I would have asked for a special news report read by Dan Rather, my favorite anchorman.

Why would I want to order a nightmare? Because there are those who claim that what one experiences in a nightmare never comes to be, never happens in reality. That is good and sufficient reason for me to have ordered this specific nightmare.

Here is the "cauchemar" I would have ordered:

"Good morning, Ladies and Gentlemen. This is Dan Rather reporting. We interrupt regular programming to bring you this special news bulletin. Last night, Mr. Howard Holloway, the most influential member of the Senate of these United States was shot dead on the Caribbean Island of Saint Martin.

"Mr. Holloway and his wife were on vacation on this small island where President Bush and French President Mr. Mitterrand were scheduled to meet later this month. The Senator and his wife were returning to their hotel after having a late dinner. According to Mrs. Holloway, who is hospitalized in Saint Thomas, the Senator stopped his car when he saw what he thought was an accident. When the Senator got out of his car to inquire and see if he could be of any assistance, three men, who hooded themselves quickly, forced him into their car, and drove him and Mrs. Holloway to a deserted beach. There, the criminals demanded money and all the jewelry the couple was wearing. The Senator refused to comply. A scuffle ensued and the Senator was shot dead. Mrs. Holloway went into shock and spent two hours alone on the deserted beach. A motorist found her later walking aimlessly on a nearby road and drove her to the police station in Philipsburg, the capital of the Dutch part of the island. After a period of confusion and procrastination, she was flown to a hospital on the nearby island of Saint Thomas, one of the U.S. Virgin Islands.

"A team of U.S. investigators has been dispatched to Saint Martin to investigate the slaying of the Senator. The State Department has confirmed that President Bush has contacted President Mitterrand of France, and has informed him that he will not meet him in Saint Martin, the French side of the island.

"Our special reporter on the scene has informed us that based on interviews he has had with numerous citizens of this small but economically booming island, both sides of the island have been plagued by a rash of murders, rapes, assaults, break-and-entries, and shootouts. Local governments have not taken the necessary steps to counter this rising tide of violence and crime.

"It is reported that the situation is such on this tiny island that it is indeed the rare businessman who does not arm himself at home, at his place of business or in his car when he travels at night. A vast majority of the islanders, who are peaceful, law-abiding people, has been complaining about the situation for quite some time, but it appears that the strategy of the local governments has been one of hushing reports of crimes committed on Saint Martin for fear that such information would negatively impact the island's tourist-based economy.

"That is all the information we have on this item. Stay

tuned to your local CBS radio stations for any update on the murder of the Senator.

Let us pray any such disaster will not come to be, but prayers alone will not suffice. Our elected officials must take concrete steps to protect law-abiding citizens from the criminals who prey on them. They, and we, the people of this island, must believe in the wisdom contained in the two sentences most of us see almost every day. One reads: "Truth never misses the road; it is only falsehood that finds itself a hole." The other: "Hide nothing from the people."

# A Mammoth "Mammouth?"*

(*The Chronicle*, December 14, 1989)

For Pastor John (Johnny) Gibbons

Marxism, Leninism and communism are moribund. Some even claim they are dead. "Dead as nail heads," they say. I think not. I say the nails still need to be struck hard, to be driven flush. Marxist-Leninist communism was a "big-grass-piece-fire." Now, all that is left of it are a few "live spots" here and there, amid scorched fields and smouldering ashes.

Fidel Castro, Manuel Ortega, and a few other super egotists continue on their trek towards that phase of the revolution, the phase that never arrives, the phase they know will never come. These men have the power, they have the ability to influence their people, but rather than concede that they erred, they persist in their egotistical lunacy, never mind the misery, destruction and death they cause.

Such men are not demented, they are not misguided; they are evil men, evil to the very core of their being. But as sure as the sun must sink into the sea over Anguilla late this afternoon, these egomaniacs, these tyrants and their henchmen will soon go under. Yes! Everything is for a time. All men must pass on, even Fidel.

Looking back at the phenomenon, at this three-headed beast called Marxist-Leninist communism, one wonders how such simplistic, such primitive interpretations of human nature, of matter, and of western history, could have inflamed the minds of so many, infecting entire generations to such a degree.

I like to think of Marxist-Leninist communism as a huge, dull square building constructed by a few master egotists; all males and western-educated persons convinced beyond the shadow of a doubt that they had the only key to the only door that led to the only room that contained the only blueprint which mapped out the only possible explanation of human nature, of the history of the West, and their interconnections; their dialectics.

Thank heaven, the people of this Island were never attracted to the beast, to the Manichean monster called communism. We were, and we remain, inoculated against any such animal. We could sense, we could feel, the blasphemous arrogant pride of its doctrine that equates the teachings of Christ and other great religious leaders with opium, opium that stupefies and kills. A doctrine that lumps those who worship with decadent opium-eaters stood no chance, stands no chance, with us.

The Swiss-born French writer, Jean-Jacques Rousseau, believed that inequality began when the first man fenced in some land then declared, "This is my property. This belongs to me." Rousseau was a genius, but even a genius can err from time to time. The American poet Robert Frost saw things somewhat differently. He recognized the important role that walls and fences play as stabilizers, as agents of order, in all societies. He argued that "good walls make good neighbors." The theoreticians of communism are much closer to Rousseau.

Yes! Communism is dying, the beast is almost dead, but what is the next "ism" on the horizon? What is the next phenomenon that will take the place of international communism, infect future generations and spread disorder, destruction and death? Will it be, might it be, international capitalism?

The international communists, the super socialists, saw the world as one huge community of classless worker-consumers. The economists and marketing strategists, who are the theoreticians of the international capitalists, reason and act not much differently from the communists. They pretend that borders, nationalities and differences do not exist. The world, for them, is one huge supermarket, a mammoth "mammouth" where fortunes are made and passports are irrelevant.

The international capitalists are forging ahead, never mind the traditions, the mother tongues, the religions. Never mind those who, like René Girard, keep reminding us that differences are essential, that order, as we know it today, is a function of the interplay, of the dialectics of differences, and that disorder sets in with the confusion brought about by the perception of a loss of differences.

**\*Mammouth**: (French for "mammoth") was the name of a recently established supermarket on the French side of Saint Martin.

# Specificity and the Siamese Twins

(*The Chronicle,* December 25, 1989)

To the Memories of Mayor Élie Fleming and Mayor Hubert Petit and for Mayor Albert Fleming

Given the important event we witnessed on Saturday, December 16, namely the visit to our homeland by the presidents of two major world powers, given such an unprecedented event, I could not resist making the Bush-Mitterrand summit the subject of my rambling.

I have read various editorials in the local press, as well as the comments of some citizens who were asked by the media to voice their opinion of the visit. I have read the comments of Senator Claude Wathey in *The Chronicle* of December 19 as well as the remarks of Mayor Albert Fleming in *The Guardian* of December 19. Last, but not least, I have read, very closely, an interesting and somewhat strange article in the prestigious, influential, usually well-informed and reliable French newspaper *Le Monde.*

This December 15 article (on the eve of the summit) does to Saint-Martin/Sint Maarten what the December 18 cover article in *Time* magazine does to the Netherland Antilles. We are getting it from both ends, on two continents, in two languages. Saint-Martin/Sint Maarten, the Franco-
Dutch Island is dubbed "The Island of all the pirates…"

In our local press and among the people of this island, there seems to be a consensus that the visit is of great importance for the island and its people. "Historic" is the word that keeps surfacing, but there has been little or no attempt at explaining the reason or reasons which might underline the selection, the choice, of this meeting place.

Why would the President of France invite the President of the United States of America to meet him for a talk in Saint-Martin/Sint Maarten? Yes! They came to this island, to both sides! Given where they landed, those who greeted them, the air space they used, the roads they traveled, etc., how can anyone claim that they only came to Saint-Martin? But the question still remains: Why would the French bypass metropolitan France, Guadeloupe, Martinique, French Guyana, etc. and select this island for their chat with President Bush?

I have no crystal ball, no special contacts here or abroad, but I try to read the unwritten text that lies between the lines. This outside text, this "hors text" is almost always more revealing than the so-called real, manifest written text.

It is obvious to most of us that there is a new world order in the making. By that I mean that the balance of power in the world is shifting and shifting fast. These are unstable, dangerous times. I am referring to power based upon military might, military power.

The U.S.S.R is disintegrating; it is falling apart. One by one, its satellites are departing. Not only are they deserting, one of them, namely East Germany is demanding reunification with its cousin state, West Germany.

The reunification of Germany is a new spice, an unpredicted, unwanted, unwelcome condiment that is spoiling the pot of fish stew for some. It is spoiling the "bouillabaisse," the great dream of a European Common Market.

Suddenly, the French, who are usually cold towards the U.S.A., are great friends of Uncle Sam. The Americans, who were being kept out (by the French) of talks related to the Common Market, are now being solicited (by the French) to play an active role. The Bush administration has taken the French bait. We must now wait and see.

But what do all these faraway European and American concerns have to do with us little folk? Here is how and where there might be some connection: According to the article in *Le Monde*, in a few years (1992?), Saint-Martin "should" (the journalist uses the conditional tense "devrait") be fully legally integrated into the European Common Market ("intégrée de plein droit").

The major problem with this integration is that the Dutch part of the island, an associate member of the Common Market since 1964, does not have to abide by the rules set by the Common Market. Another problem, according to this *Le Monde* article, is that Mayor Albert Fleming and his team have been trying for some time to secure special status for Saint-Martin, a status that would maintain the close relationship with France while going much further in allowing for the special relationship with Dutch Sint Maarten and the specificity of this Island.

The article in *Le Monde* is not anything we can be proud of. It is a hard-hitting article wherein "Saint-Martin" is dragged over the coals. There are references to offshore companies, drug trafficking, and runaway destructive investment in the construction of hotels destined to remain vacant. According to *Le Monde,* this island is "the paradise for smugglers and racketeers."

Given the tone and substance of this article, and given the cover article of *Time* magazine, the meeting of Presidents Bush and Mitterrand on this island could be a master diplomatic move on the part of the French, a move designed to send several more-or-less subtle messages to different individuals and/or groups.

For Mayor Albert Fleming, it could be a demonstration; a warning that this French government does not intend to lie down and play dead while he and his team dictate some special relationship with France and French policy towards the European Common Market.

For Senator Claude Wathey, who for some time now has been dreaming of a more united "Saint-Martin," this display of French-American dialogue and of French presence in the region might serve as warning that the road to independence is not as clear as he may think.

For the Americans, whose president must fear for his safety in these Americas while the President of France mingles with the people, this could be a demonstration, a reminder, that France is present and respected in the Caribbean, especially in the Northern Caribbean. She is present exactly where it (the U.S.A.) might need diplomatic support, if not France's assistance, in the war against drug traffickers and money-launderers: "the Siamese Twins," the two number-one policy items in American domestic and international politics.

History is testimony to the fact that the U.S.A. and a number of European nations have not hesitated, will not hesitate, to use the islands of the Caribbean and the people of these lands as bargaining chips in their quest for what they consider higher, nobler pursuits in Europe, North America or elsewhere.

Président Mitterrand and
Mayor Albert Fleming in 1989

# What Happens if We Win?

(*The Chronicle*, January 3, 1990)

For Angèle, Jacqueline and Joseph Daniel

This week, my rambling took me to Marigot, where, over a buddy's lime punch, I had the great pleasure of putting a few questions to my mentor and friend Professor Theodore Lowi, who is visiting with his relatives for the holidays.

Dr. Lowi is John L. Senior Professor of American Institutions in the Department of Government at Cornell University. A graduate of Yale University (Ph.D. 1961), Dr. Lowi was on the faculty of the University of Chicago and of Columbia University prior to going to Cornell where he has been since 1972. He is the author of several books and numerous articles. His award-winning book, *The End of Liberalism*, is required reading for students of American Institutions and Government.

Theodore Lowi is no stranger to this island. Since his marriage to the former Angèle Daniel of Marigot in 1963, there has evolved a special connection with the island, with its people, and their fate or destiny. Professor Lowi's first visit dates back to 1969, some twenty years ago. Since then, he has been a frequent and regular visitor to Saint-Martin/Sint Maarten. Dr. Lowi is also quite familiar with the institutions and government of modern France. He has spent several years lecturing and doing research in Paris, where, incidentally, he will be returning in a few days.

In view of all of the above, I felt it would be interesting and enlightening to have a sort of chat with this distinguished scholar.

G. Hunt: - Professor Lowi, I've prepared a few questions I would like to put to you during this sort of interview. I would like to thank you, in advance, for having accepted to answer these questions. The first one is as follows: This Island is and is not the island you first visited in 1969. On this, the twentieth anniversary of your first visit, how would you respond to such a statement?

T. Lowi: - I'm more struck by the differences than by the continuity. The island now is a prosperous, bustling, industrialized modern metropolis, whereas in 1969 it was much more laid-back, much more of a tropical island, much more distinctive, different from the metropolis of the U.S. and France. So, I'm much more struck by the differences than by the continuity.

G. Hunt: - There are Saint Martiners, both French and Dutch Antilleans, who believe this island should be independent, its people more unified with English as their official language, and with some kind of closer connection and/or political link with the U.S.A. Assuming those wishes are fulfilled, what might result from any such status?

T. Lowi: - I question the premise itself, the idea that this island can be both independent and unified in the context you have outlined. I think unification and independence do not necessarily go hand in hand. Not that they cannot go together, but it would take an awful lot of hard work to make it possible, a lot of impositions in order to bring about unification and independence at once and together. Before one can gauge the advantages or disadvantages of any such status, one has to question whether independence and unification can occur together.

I think that, in the case outlined, unification would come at the expense of independence. If there is unification, it will come in the form of an industrialized, western capitalist island. So the unification and the independence would simply be one of becoming an undifferentiated part, a particle of an international capitalist economy. By the way, when I use the word "capitalism," I use it completely objectively. Very often, capitalism is a favorite word used by Marxists. I'm not a Marxist, I'm a Liberal, and, by and large, very favorable to free market operations, but I'm not ready to blind myself to the price that one pays to join an international economy in which the players are enormously large multi-national corporations. So one looks to the cost, in terms, not of people becoming poorer, because prosperity might flow from independence, but the cost can come from having to lose one's uniqueness as a society, as a people.

G. Hunt: - You have read the document titled "The project for Saint-Martin" wherein a new status for Saint-Martin is proposed and outlined. Would you have any comments you might care to share with us with regard to this document?

T. Lowi: - The document is eloquent. I'm impressed with its rhetoric and with the strength of its commitment, but I think the document is significant, more for what it does not say than for what it states. It ties together ambitiously the proposal for a special relationship to France and the Common Market. It ties that special relationship to a very ambitious plan of construction and reconstruction of Saint Martin, but what's absent from it is the means by which all of this is to occur, and I'm very dubious about this aspect. I don't see how all of that can be accomplished with the revision of status. Saint Martin would surely gain something from a move towards direct relationship with Paris, unmediated by Guadeloupe. I think that this island has always been a loser in having to go through Guadeloupe.

Much is left unsaid in this document, and I suspect that as one gets closer to 1993, these unsaid elements will surface in the form of problems which will have to be dealt with, will have to be looked at closely. Two things are most significant in their absence from this document. One is that there is very little or nothing said about the relationship with Dutch Saint Martin, and the other is that the document does not speak of the heavy taxation that must inevitably be required to accomplish the very ambitious project that it outlines.

G. Hunt: - To end this interview, is there anything you might like to add, any question I have not put forth that you may wish to ask yourself and answer for the benefit of Saint Martiners?

T. Lowi: - If I had to stress anything, it would be in connection with what we have discussed, and it would be the distinction between the economic and the political. By political, I don't mean just running for office, I mean political in the broader sense, in the sense of the ancient Greeks, in the sense that you, Gerard, understand and appreciate. If I could stress anything, it would be the runaway quality of the local leadership, that they are so crazy about growth, they have gone crazy over growth to such an extent that they are not stopping and asking themselves the more fundamental questions: What happens if we win? What happens if we succeed in a larger, more prosperous island? Would there be anything here worth sustaining? So my concern is that this island is becoming a client of the U.S.A. I'm not anti-U.S. I'm an American citizen. I'm a loyal American, but my concern is that to become a direct client of the U.S. is to lose an identity forged over centuries.

While France offers a great deal of burden—France is an old-fashioned and somewhat burdensome, heavy handed State—there are certain qualities about France. France is concerned about capitalism. Even now that France is no longer dominated by Marxist thinking, France still has an ancient State that is concerned about eternal virtues. It may make mistakes, but I think that if I were an islander looking around for some country that my island can become a client of, for some larger partner to protect me, I think I would still prefer France.

I think that "The Project for Saint-Martin" is in the right direction. Becoming a client of the U.S.A. means becoming a client of international banking, international tourism, international air companies, and multinational corporations, and that's not a country. You'll be becoming simply a unit, a part in a very large international system that doesn't care about your water, your land or your people. It can't care. It can only care about one thing, about the bottom line, about profit. That's a terrible relationship to have.

G. Hunt: - Professor Lowi, I thank you kindly.

# Sponges?

(*The Chronicle*, January 17, 1990)

For Aline Choisy and Evelyne Fleming

When one sets about thinking, writing, speaking of this island, and its "one people," one of the first major difficulties one encounters is a problem of naming, of designating, of defining, of saying; a fundamental problem of language, of being, and of belonging, or rather, a problem of language-being-belonging.

We are a people with many identities, and we claim each one so fervently that we are lost in the confusion, in the proliferation of names. We have so many names that we can barely say who we are. We are looking for one name among all these names, an identity we can answer to the way most others do when they say, "We are from Amsterdam, we are Dutch, we speak Dutch" or "We are from Lyon, we are French, we speak French." Notice how the Dutch and French designate both the nationality and the mother tongue.

We, the so-called "one people" are from Sint Maarten, or Saint-Martin, or Saint Marten, or North Saint-Martin or South Saint Martin, etc. I will spare you the various abbreviations thereof. Officially, some are Dutch Antilleans, with Dutch as their official language. Others are French Antilleans, with French as their official language.

Unofficially, at home, with our family, and in our everyday lives, the overwhelming majority of us speak English, our English. Never mind those who claim that they can barely understand us. We understand each other, and those with whom we do business understand us.

When I say that we are "one people," I am not implying that only this one people live on the island. It is obvious that there are many other persons living among us, other Antilleans, Europeans, Asians, Americans, Canadians, etc. The "one people" designates those islanders whose roots are in this island.

This claim to some difference, some specificity, some priority, should not offend anyone, but it can, it does, and I sense that soon this reference to the "one people" will become more offensive to some residents who might feel excluded. We are not quite there as yet, but given the trend in the immigration onto this island, the time is almost here already when we will have to say that the "one people" live among the new immigrants.

I have the privilege—yes, indeed, it's a kind of privilege—to experience firsthand in a unique, an exemplary, way, some of the feelings of estrangement, marginality and neglect that inhabit, which must inhabit, the vast majority of Saint Martiners. "Saint Martiners" is my spelling for our "one people."

I teach French at Milton Peters College, where the language of instruction and internal administration is Dutch. When official and staff meetings take place, when teachers meet to review and/or discuss the work of students, when an official of the School Board meets officially with the teaching staff, the language spoken is Dutch. One may indeed speak English at these meetings, but in order to participate fully, one must be able to understand Dutch.

As I sit in these staff meetings surrounded by an overwhelming majority of teachers from abroad, teachers who are not natives of this island but who all, to my knowledge, speak English, I have the strange feeling of being an outsider, a stranger, the way I often felt in Canada. But here, at Milton Peters College, this feeling is more acute. Here I can't even understand what is being said, here I am muted, a muted stranger in my own country. Or is this "Dutch Side," this southern part of the island, my own country?

When I exit the staff room where these official meetings are held, where most Dutch teachers naturally speak Dutch among themselves, when I exit and listen to the students in the hallway and in the schoolyard, I feel at home once again, at home in the language.

A few weeks ago, at a staff meeting, a Dutch colleague, sensing perhaps the burlesque paradox of the situation, or maybe reading the estrangement in my look, asked me how it felt to be in such a predicament. I told him that I found it somewhat difficult, that I felt out of place in the setting. But the more I search for a more descriptive answer to his question, the more I feel that short of learning Dutch quickly and well, which is not easy, even for a language teacher, one must become sponge-like.

In order to maintain one's psychic sanity, one must become light and porous, capable of soaking up incongruities and abnormalities, soaking them up, and retaining them until they may be released, expelled—hopefully without there remaining too much acid residue in the "chambers" of one's psyche.

Let there be no misunderstanding here, no misreading. I have no score to settle with my School Board, with my Directors at School, or with my colleagues at Milton Peters College. Officials of the School Board, Directors at my school, and fellow teachers, have all been very "correct" with me. Some colleagues have even interpreted for me at some meetings. I trust they will appreciate (in the true sense of the word "appreciate") the point I am trying to make here, which has to do with a procedure they did not institute.

I must also emphasize that "systemic" situations that foster the kind of estrangement and alienation I am trying to address here are, in my view, much more prevalent, much more blatant on the French Side of this island. There, language and institutional administrative barriers isolate the native English-speaking Saint Martiner. There, it is impossible for a St. Martiner from the Dutch Side to secure employment in the French public school system.

In my article "Of Language-Being" a few weeks ago, I tried to reflect on the benefits we reap from our polymorphism. I referred to the specificity it bestows on us, the advantages being able to speak several languages accords us, to the difficulties inherent in any modification, any change, of the system. However, must we persist in alienating ourselves in order to maintain this polymorphic specificity? Can we not teach mathematics, geography, history, physics, French, Dutch, Spanish, etc. in our schools and, at the same time "be at home in English" in these schools?

English is the glue, the cement, the main ingredient, that connects and binds St. Martiners into one people on this tiny, this minuscule, island, the only place on Mother Earth they can really call home.

Is it not time we put an end to our mimicry, our propensity for losing ourselves by melting into others— the French, the Dutch? Is it not time we come home to our native tongue?

When we visit others, we must try hard to speak their language, but at home we must speak amongst ourselves in our language, lest the estrangement, the alienation, persist and increase and one day soon we cease being sponge-*like* and become sponges.

# Home, at Last?

(*The Chronicle*, January 24, 1990)

For Daniella Jeffry-Pilot and Josiane Artsen Fleming

"-He is a disgrace to this family, a damn disgrace. He is running after this woman who is horning him in clear daylight. The boy is a disgrace, I tell you, a disgrace to his mother, to his father, to all of us in this family. He is such a nice-looking boy! He can have any woman, any woman he want, but no! He only want her, and she is horning him, and he is going around, telling everybody how he love her still, how he need her, and how he is lost without her. Now you tell me, tell me Gé, you ever hear so much damn stupidness?"

-No! I said to the older man, as I stared at the ground like a boy afraid of being caught telling a lie. But, yes! Yes, I thought, that's all we hear, all we've been hearing, and for such a long time. But I don't think that he is stupid for standing firm and saying that he loves this woman; that he still loves her despite all those things you say she has done and is still doing. No! He is not disgracing himself and his family by admitting that he still loves her. How can you disgrace yourself or others by saying you love someone?

But my older friend had already made up his mind. He had convinced himself. He would not suffer any contradiction, any dissension, not now, not here. I'll talk with him later, I thought. Some other day when I'll have time to stay a while and chat; when he'll have cooled off somewhat; when I'll have searched and found a better way, a better tone of voice in which to say all I felt so suddenly but did not, could not, say. All of this brings me to Lasana M. Sekou and his *Love Songs Make You Cry*.

In writing, speaking, loving, the tone of one's voice is almost always more important than the message that is carried. For whatever it is worth, I agree with my friend Daniella Jeffry, that *Love Songs Make You Cry* brings forth a "change of technique, an evolution, and a meaningful contribution" to the fledgling literature of this island.

Yes! Sekou has come home at last, home to a form we recognize, a discourse that is authentic, to a voice that is comforting. Now we may listen to stories that are not only "his" stories but also "histories—our stories." Now, winds of anger and dissent driven by desire are abating and shifting. Now Sekou may have sensed a rule of life itself, where all things unite through love and are torn apart by strife. From this, he may have gathered that a poet's task is to gauge the ebb and flow of love and hate in their inextricable struggle, and to always side with victims...

> Fatty, you taking all tha' money home, (...)
> You giving it away you know. Everybody could
> see you growing horns, you must be blind ...
> Somebody else must be taking your place...
> (Page 26)

Julie hits Fatty, a St.-Martiner, where it hurts most—in his concept of manliness, his machismo. Sekou's narrator helps us experience the pain, the overwhelming suffering that Julie inflicts on Fatty:

> Every word, like a fang, like a claw, like a machete, bit into Fatty, jabbed into Fatty, poked into Fatty, slashed at Fatty, cut poor Fatty down to size bad... (Page 26)

One day, instead of going to work, Fatty spends hours in the hot ceiling of his house, waiting, "cooping" his woman, Annie. He had to know, to see for himself, if Julie and those who had been making fun of him were right. He had to verify if Annie was "horning" him.

When Fatty heard his woman making love with another man in the bedroom that his labor had built,

> Fatty rose up like a raging bull and butt his head on the rafters. He cried out in pain and anguish. The mad bull dug one hoof down and the ceiling gave way... (Page 28)

All is well that ends well. Many years later, Fatty, who had followed Annie to New Jersey to "fix her good," returns to "sweet S'maatin" with his wife Annie and their children, and they both look back and laugh at their past.

This funny little story is not as innocent as it might appear on a superficial reading. Sekou's narrator is hard, hard indeed, on those who enjoy causing others to suffer:

The assassin sat there, a wicked smile of contentment twisted her face into a stroke. How ugly she was now, raged Fatty inside himself. Crush her, he thought. Crush all who inflict pain on others... (Page 26)

"Fatty and the Big House" is but one of the five short stories of *Love Songs Make You Cry*. All five are captivating songs of love and hatred. Read them quickly; it's later than you think.

# Syllogisms of Despair?

(*The Chronicle*, February 7, 1990)

For Alain Richardson, Louis Mussington and all former members of SMECO

Poseidon, the Greek god of the sea and of earthquakes, lived in the depths of the ocean. He was armed with a trident—not the chewing gum, but a three-pronged spear. He could control the waves, shatter rocks and shake the shores. He was also the ruler of springs (the water supply), which he turned on and off at will.

Poseidon, like all powerful Greek gods, didn't hesitate to chastise giants and lower ranking gods who defied him and his pals. Legend has it that one day, Polybotes, an upstart giant, decided to defy Poseidon. Poseidon, who was well known for his violence, got angry. Polybotes started running, or rather swimming. The chase led them close to the island of Cos. Poseidon, without giving it a second thought, grabbed a piece of this island, tore it off, and threw it at Polybotes, burying poor Polybotes beneath the rubble.

Some wise folks claim that myths are there so that we may give full reign to our imagination. We must leave poor Polybotes beneath his rubble.

POSEIDOM (with an "m" instead of and "n") is an acronym. It stands for « Programme d'Options Spécifiques à l'Éloignement et à l'Insularité des Départements d'Outre-Mer ». This might be rendered in English as "Program of Specific Options to Cope with the Remoteness and the Insularity of the Overseas Departments" (in order to incorporate them into the European Economic Community or EEC.)

I like to think of problems as questions. The answer one arrives at is a function of the question one asks. It is obvious that the question put forth by the European members of the committee that instituted or established POSEIDOM is none other than the following: "How can the overseas departments (of France) be incorporated into the EEC?"

Thus, from the very beginning, the fundamental democratic right of the people of these overseas departments, their right to self-determination, is negated, and the enquiry, the process itself, is vitiated. This is a direct result of the incredible attitude of this French government, and of all French governments to date, with respect to the relationship between France and its overseas departments.

As incredible as it may sound, all governments of France since 1946 have maintained that the overseas Caribbean departments are integral parts of metropolitan France. France is, of course, a European community, and since the Caribbean departments are integral parts of France, these islands are European communities as well. The problem with this exercise in deduction is the obvious fact that the premise is invalid—invalid to everyone but to French governments. Caribbean islands are simply not, they can never be, "integral parts of metropolitan France."

The inquiry is vitiated, for it is taken for granted that the people of Guadeloupe, Martinique, French Guyana, and, of course, Saint-Martin, wish their island to be incorporated into the EEC. That is why the question that is put is: "How can incorporation/integration be accomplished?" Not the question: "Should these lands be incorporated into the EEC?"

Had the committee that formulated POSEIDOM begun with the latter question, they would have had to conclude that it is the people of these lands who must decide whether or not they wished to be incorporated into the EEC.

When one reads the "Projet de Décision Commune du Conseil et de la Commission instituant POSEIDOM," a preliminary draft –of the Committee that formulated POSEIDOM it becomes obvious that this committee of Europeans, piloted by French officials, saw no reason for consulting the people of the French Overseas' Departments or DOM. That is why the first chapter of the draft: "La Situation des DOM" (the status of the Overseas Departments) is entitled "Leur appartenance à l'Europe," literally: "their state/nature/situation of belonging to Europe" ("appartenance," from "appartenir," to belong to). This might seem incredible, but it is there for anyone to verify. An entire exposé is then put forward explaining how/why they "belong" to France and, consequently, to Europe.

I have searched religiously for the name "Saint-Martin" in the 40-page decision instituting POSEIDOM, this joint report prepared by European officials, but "Saint-Martin" is nowhere to be found.

Representatives of the French government will argue that even though it is not there, it is still there; that Saint-Martin is Guadeloupe, Guadeloupe is France, France is Europe, and therefore, Saint-Martin is Europe. If you believe this, then tomorrow morning drive up to the Fort Hill, walk into the "Sous-Préfecture," ask to see the "Sous-Préfet," and insist that you must drive to Paris, but that all the roads are blocked.

In a remarkable speech delivered January 29, 1989, Mr. Louis-Constant Fleming, Regional Councillor of Saint-Martin, in response to POSEIDOM, argued eloquently that Saint-Martin will be struck a fatal blow if POSEIDOM is implemented. Mr. Aimé Césaire, the great poet and the Deputy of Martinique, has warned that his people will not accept the POSEIDOM, that there must be a referendum on the question of integration into the EEC. The people of Guadeloupe are equally alarmed, but the officials of this so-called socialist government will not listen; they cannot hear.

We must not conclude that all the French governments since 1946, all those French officials, were/are incompetent simpletons. France has produced, and continues to produce, some of the greatest minds, and French government officials are highly educated persons. The French education system is one the best there is. No, we must look elsewhere for an answer to this obstinacy, this persistence, this single-minded determination on the part of all French governments, to own us; to insist that we are not different; to deny us our difference, our specificity; to strangle us in their embrace.

France is a nation obsessed with the idea of "puissance," of "grandeur," with the idea of power and eminence. We live in the backyard of the still mighty U.S.A. French diplomats have developed an art of using these islands of the Caribbean as bargaining chips in their quest for glory and other more earthly pursuits in their dealings with Uncle Sam.

Given all of the above, and given the deadlock we have reached, with 1992 at our threshold, with a violent POSEIDOM swimming our way, is it not time we drew a big red line (in ink, not blood), time we stand up firmly but peacefully and demand that our specificity be respected, that our difference be recognized?

Isn't it high time we stop the feuding which saps our energy, disperses our concentration, dividing and weakening us, reducing us to silent puffs of air, muted adversaries in this all-important, vital, crucial debate wherein our opponents are masters, our masters?

# Language – Justice

For Evelyne Fléming and Sonia Fléming

The St. Maarten's "Association for Supervision and Curriculum Development" (ASCD) invited me to participate in their "Panel Discussion on Bilingual Education" of February 21, 1990 along with four other individuals: Mrs. Daniella Jeffry, Mrs. Rita Rassion, Mr. Wycliffe Smith and Mr. Reynold Groeneveldt. At the very last minute, after I had prepared my presentation, I was asked to fill in as moderator and informed that I could still make the presentation I had already prepared as a member of the panel. I saw no problem with that arrangement and I accepted. "Of Language-Justice" was read at that "Discussion." Two days later, on February 23, the text appeared in *The Chronicle*.

One of the paradoxes of life is what I call "the paradox of language." Of course, all paradoxes are rooted in language since, by definition, a paradox is an opinion, a proposition. What are opinions, propositions, if not spoken/written language? In logic, a paradox is a proposition that is both true and false. The paradox most often cited is the paradox of the liar. When a liar states that he is lying while telling his lie, he is also not lying since he is telling the truth while lying.

A paradox is also an opinion that is contrary to the opinion that prevails, contrary to the opinion commonly held. This latter definition, this paradox, is the one I am referring to when I speak of "the paradox of language." Language, the spoken/written word, has a way of fooling us into believing, of having us believe, of inciting us to believe, that this planet Earth, this world of mind and matter we inhabit, is not One and Becoming, but a multitude of separate, stagnant entities. Ordinary language, as opposed to great art, great poetry, and above all, great music, cannot deal adequately with the "becoming," the never-ending flux, or with the interconnections, the dialectics of life and the universe. Language, ink marks on virgin paper, noises breaking up a silence, words written and spoken, aim to "re-present," to restore to a previous condition, to "bring back" something that is absent. Such is the nature, the limits, of ordinary language.

Tonight, my topic is "Culture, language and education." Look at the print, the ink marks: the words on the program outline. Listen to me voice these terms: "Culture, language and education." Almost right away, one gets the impression that we are dealing with three entities, three separate, disconnected concepts. That is the tricking I refer to, the fooling. We go along thinking that we master language, but all the time it is language that is mastering us.

We must be watchful. We must be cognizant of this built-in aspect of language, of the limits and limitation of the spoken/written word.

I was asked, we were asked, to insure that each presentation be relevant to the topic assigned to us. I will try to comply with this request, but for the sake of argument,

I have added the word "justice" to the three nouns I was asked to discuss. Let us then begin with justice and try to make our way to "language-culture-education."

A dictionary is almost always a good way to begin when dealing with words. My dictionary, *Le Petit Robert,* a good French dictionary, informs me that justice is "a moral principle to which the law tries to conform." It adds that justice can also mean "the organization responsible for the administration of laws, laws enacted in accordance with the moral principle."

So I learned from my dictionary, that justice is a moral principle; that some people make laws in accordance with this principle; that "justice" can mean these laws and the system that enforces them. But have you noticed that my dictionary still has not really explained what justice is? It did not tell me what this moral principle is. My dictionary referred me to another word, to the word "moral." When I looked up the meaning of moral, I learned that moral has its origin in 13th century Europe and comes from a Latin word meaning "that which concerns the habits, the customs, and specifically, the rules of behaviour of a society." I learned that "moral" and "ethical" are synonymous and are concerned with "the good" and "the bad," but I still need to know, precisely, what is "good" and what is "bad." I'm still looking for a way to get it right, to get "justice" right; to draw a red line and say, "There! That is "justice."

Of course, there is no end, and if I look up the word "good," its definition will refer me to another word; it will put off my inquiry. As they say in French, "la réponse sera différée, remise." Indeed, the answer is always deferred, put off. As Jacques Derrida and others before and after him have taught us, this is the nature of language. Language comes about and sustains itself through the interplay of differences and deferment. Language mimics life, but this mimicry, like all mimicry, is, of course, never perfect; it is a "re-presentation," one that is always incomplete, always lacking. Language, ordinary language, is indeed a poor mime, a poor mimic.

We humans are, in effect, the sum of what we say, write and do. We are, therefore, "caught up," so to speak, with language in this serious game of deferment and repetition. On the other hand, we long for completion, finality, the end, the conclusion. We seek the solid rock on which to stand and feel secure. Therefore, we go about saying and believing that we have finished this or that, that we have written the definitive study on this or that. But do we really ever finish anything? Can we truly write a definitive study of something?

This does not mean that we must forget about trying to get things "right," that we must stop trying to improve our system of education, for example. To the contrary, we absolutely need to draw red lines and to act, to take action based on our conclusions which are always provisional. We must stand ready to erase our red lines, our boundaries, to move them forward or backward, up or down, right or left. We must recognize the incomplete nature of all conclusions and the overwhelming priority of the question over the answer.

When we recognize this important, fundamental aspect of language, we also recognize that language permeates all concepts, all ideas, since language is the expression of our thoughts. Language is, therefore, inseparable from education, culture, politics, economics, marketing, love, madness, etc., etc. All concepts are inconceivable without language, inconceivable outside of language.

No, I have not forgotten justice. Is justice possible outside of language? Is justice possible without language? In a democracy, people are supposed to listen to candidates speak, read what candidates write, observe how candidates live, then choose, select, some of these candidates to represent them, re-present them, that is, to make them—the people—present in their absence. In office, the primary responsibility of these elected representatives is to serve the people in keeping with their mandate and to formulate and enact laws to govern their society.

Before a bill becomes law, it is written and debated. Without language, without the spoken/written word, there can be no bill, no laws, no peace, no justice; no civilized society. Instead, there is discord, strife, disorder, violence, injustice, anarchy.

It is with language, through language, communication, the spoken/written word, that people are able to live a relatively peaceful life in society. It is through language that we get justice, which is the key ingredient of a healthy society. Justice is, therefore, not an isolated concept. There are no isolated concepts, not even the concept isolation.

Justice is a derivative, a by-product, of language itself and of relationships.

I hope you have noticed what happened here tonight. We went in search of justice and we found her everywhere, inseparable from language, inextricably linked to language. Yes! I like to think of justice as a "she," the way the French, the Spanish and some others do.

Of course, you may have noticed that I did not make my way to "culture and education" or "love and madness," etc., but I hope the trail I made is wide enough and clear enough, and that, from where I am stopping here, you can see them clearly up ahead, inextricably linked to Lady Justice and, therefore, to language.

# Syllogisms for a Dialogue?

(Part 1 of 3 parts)

(*The Chronicle*, March 7, 1990)

For Gracita Arrindell

On Monday, February 26, 1990, the speech titled "If Implementation of English is not Planned, it Will Happen by Default" by Mr. Wycliffe Smith (then Educational Advisor to the Executive Council) was published in the Chronicle. This is a speech he had read at the "Panel Discussion" of February 21, 1990. My "Syllogisms for a Dialogue?" must be placed and viewed in that context.

It is good to meet and discuss problems, be they actual or potential. The question of the language of instruction in the public schools of Saint Maarten is of primordial, vital interest to every citizen of this Island-Territory, whether he or she recognizes it as such or not.

As a teacher, a St. Martiner who, to date, has spent most of his adult life teaching in a so-called bilingual country, namely Canada, I believe that I might have some ideas, a perspective that might help to advance the present dialogue on the language of instruction.

By referring to Canada as a "so-called bilingual country," I wish to indicate that even though Canada, this great country, has two official languages (French and English), although there is official bilingualism at the Federal level, Canada is still far from being a truly bilingual country.

Bilingual education is alive and faring more or less well in only three of the ten provinces. In the Northwest Territories and in the seven other provinces, English reigns supreme, with exceptions. In the northern areas, native people speak their languages, which some pundits still refer to as "dialects."

Although the format of the February 21$^{st}$ Panel Discussion on Bilingual Education sponsored by the ASCD was not the most conducive to the kind of serious dialogue warranted by such an important issue, any such attempt at airing this vital subject must be encouraged. The St. Maarten ASCD should be commended for its initiative and encouraged to continue its efforts.

When such meetings take place, participating panelists and the press (the printed media in particular) should ensure that the various points of view expressed at such meetings are published in order that educators, representatives of the people, parents and other competent individuals can study the arguments and contribute to this major dialogue.

On February 26, *The Chronicle* published the speech delivered by Mr. Wycliffe Smith at the February 21st Panel Discussion. Using mostly outdated data (latest study cited dates back to 1974) and citing mainly American researchers who are not at all the leading researchers on bilingualism, Mr. Smith undertakes a seemingly exhaustive survey of the various programs. We are treated to a lot of the terminology that is so characteristic of professors of education: "Transitional Bilingualism," "Monoliterate…," "Partial Biliterate…," "Full Biliterate…," "The Immersion Model," "The Submersion Model," all such jargon which, to a great extent, has prompted the commissions and committees investigating the abysmal state of teacher education in the U.S. to recommend that American universities close their faculties of education.

After demonstrating to us that he has read some research done sixteen years ago, Mr. Smith concludes his argument where he might have begun it, by rejecting all of these approaches and arguing that "a bilingual education system is totally out of place on this island."

Like Mr. Smith, I believe that it would be more appropriate to make English the language of instruction throughout the public school system and to give Dutch priority as a second language. At the Secondary Level, Spanish, French and other languages could also be offered.

Having said this, I do not at all believe what Mr. Smith seems to take for granted—that "if implementation of English as the language of instruction is not planned, implemented by design, it will take place by default."

Given the communication explosion and specifically the advent of U.S. television on this island, given our geographical location and our historical antecedents, it is obvious that English will continue to gain ground, to reinforce and entrench itself on St. Maarten. But to my knowledge, English is not the language in which justice speaks in St. Maarten. English is not the official language, the "constitutional language" of St. Maarteners, even though the Island Council deliberates in English.

The problem with Mr. Smith's reasoning if I may put it this way is a problem common to most bureaucrats and/ or specialists: they tend to have a kind of tunnel vision, to view problems as isolates, as entities, not in their context. Mr. Smith is obviously a very educated and talented individual, but he does not see the interconnections, the inter-relationships; the dialectics of the problem. If he sees them, he has neglected to express them. He tackles neither the crux of the problem nor its overall context.

The language of instruction in the public schools is directly, intimately, inextricably linked to the language of the law of the land; the language of the courts; the language in which lawyers and notaries and civil servants speak; "the language in which judges administer justice; the language in which justice is made to express itself."

Mr. Smith's analysis does not address this aspect of the problem. By so doing, by falling short in his diagnosis, Mr. Smith runs the risk of aggravating the illness and making treatment more elusive, more complicated.

# Syllogisms for a Dialogue?

(Part 2 of 3 parts)

(*The Chronicle*, March 8, 1990)

For Henry Brookson

Any serious attempt at apprehending the language of instruction issue in St. Maarten must also address those problems which are already surfacing and which will increasingly surface, as graduates from local English language schools who have continued their education in English language universities throughout the world return home.

As these graduates return as teachers, accountants, engineers, scientists, doctors, nurses (specifically those educated in North America), they will have to contend with certain requirements imposed on them by the juridical-administrative-Dutch-Antillean-system, by a constitution they can barely read.

Major drawbacks must be anticipated for bright and gifted unilingual Anglophone St. Maarteners who will desire to pursue careers as notaries, lawyers, judges, civil servants, etc. How could they ever succeed in the present system, given the fact that Dutch is the official language in St. Maarten?

It is for these reasons that I argue that the present

dual system of education wherein some students study in Dutch language schools while others study in English language schools further exacerbates, further complicates, the already difficult issue of the language of instruction in the public schools of the land.

Something must be done to correct the situation, and it must be done soon before entire generations of young St. Maarteners are made to suffer such unfair, frustrating and impossible options as those I have tried to outline above.

In his speech delivered at the Panel Discussion on Bilingualism, Mr. Reynold Groeneveldt recognized the importance of what I like to call the "language-justice connection." He argued that given the complexity of the situation, given the problems a change from Dutch to English would bring about, given the loss of Dutch financial assistance, it is preferable to remain with Dutch as the official language of instruction, and to continue to teach English as well as other languages as second languages.

Let us consider one of the major, if not *the* major, drawback to instituting, to making, English the language of instruction in the public schools and the official language or the language of justice and administration in St. Maarten. This hurdle is that education, and higher education in particular, is a very expensive proposition, which the majority of our parents are not able to meet. Mr. Groeneveldt explained that students in the present Dutch system receive substantial, if not full, financial assistance in various forms from Holland. He anticipates that given a change-over to English as official language and language of instruction in public schools, such funds will cease to be available.

Given the enormous cost of college and graduate education in the U.S., how would most parents secure a higher education for their children? Faced with such a seemingly unsolvable problem, Mr. Groeneveldt opts for the status quo, or rather, for Dutch as the language of instruction in the public schools.

It seems that for Mr.Groeneveldt, this problem does not take a solution. For others, there may be ways of getting around this obstacle. There is, for example, the University of Saint Martin. Despite the ridicule that some are so quick to level at this fledgling, this infant, institution; this hopeful undertaking; this commendable effort; this beacon of hope, of confidence, in the future!

Notwithstanding the short-sighted criticism of those who have no confidence in themselves and, therefore, can have none in others; notwithstanding the bad faith of those who forget that all universities, even Oxford, La Sorbonne, Harvard and Leiden had beginnings and were most likely, ridiculed in their beginning, I believe that the University of St. Martin could provide a solution. This institution could go a long way in filling the void that would remain once the Dutch faucets are closed. Properly equipped and staffed, it could dispense a college education completely or partially financed by the Island Government. Mr. Groeneveldt did not even mention the University of St. Martin.

Even though I strongly disagree with Mr. Groeneveldt's

conclusions, I believe that he sees the issue or problem in a much broader context than does Mr. Smith. Having said this, I must hurry to add that Mr. Groeneveldt's charts, his educational jargon, complete with his so-called statistics and schematic diagrams, obfuscate in the same manner as Mr. Smith's seemingly exhaustive survey.

When Mr. Groeneveldt, using pseudo-scientific data, tries to prove that English is not the mother tongue of "St. Maarteners" because "most children now have Haitians and Dominicanas as nannies while their mothers work," the dialogue has degenerated far beyond debate into a realm called fantasy.

I am told that Mr. Groeneveldt is from Grand-Case. One feels like asking him in which language, in which tongue, he speaks to his folks in Grand-Case when he visits with them. Mr. Groeneveldt must exit his office and visit schoolyards, playgrounds and hallways. There, he will hear his mother tongue, our mother tongue. Of course, there are those who might argue that the mother tongue or tongues of most St. Maarteners is/are the one/ones spoken before the "middle passage," before the uprooting. While it is healthy and wise to remember the journey, the road back to these "tongues" seems, unfortunately, impossible to navigate.

# Syllogisms for a Dialogue?

(Part 3 of 3 parts)

(*The Chronicle*, March 9, 1990)

For Senator Marcel Gumbs

Given the present political status of Sint Maarten and its anticipated revised political status as a member of a kingdom of four, the language of instruction in the public schools, which is inseparable from the question of an official language of the country, needs to be viewed in a context that incorporates the positions of both Mr. Smith and Mr. Groeneveldt.

This important, this vital, dialogue should be opened up, not only to specialists in the area of education but to the entire population and specifically to the elected representatives of the people of St. Maarten. This is an urgent matter. The status quo, the dual Dutch/English system, leads to the bottleneck I have tried to outline.

Such difficult dialogue can easily degenerate into partisan debate that will only contribute in making a bad situation worse. To ask a teacher, a notary, a lawyer, a judge, a civil servant, an engineer, or an architect to consider the present Dutch system with a mind towards eliminating it and replacing it by an English system is to ask them to go against their interest. Nevertheless, I believe this is exactly what needs to be done. However, before making such a request, the parameters and the tone of the dialogue should be set forth so that these individuals, without whom any change will abort, can feel secure enough to accept the challenge that such an undertaking entails.

There are ways of ensuring that such individuals do not lose their positions in the advent of a switch from Dutch to English. There is no reason why a person who is a principal of a school, a lawyer, a notary, or any civil servant could not continue in their respective positions (with some adjustments) in a Saint Martin where English is the official language of the land and the language of instruction in the public school system.

In closing this last part of my much-too-long critique, I would like to argue against the usage of the word "independence" in the course of this vital dialogue. Independence is a "snarl" word, as opposed to a "purr" word. It is one of those pompous words which, like certain drugs, induces an artificial sense of well being and complete autonomy, a sense of elation, a belief that one can go it alone without connections, without depending on others. But there is no such thing as an independent thing. There is no person or country that is really independent. There is surely no island that is an island unto itself. There are degrees of autonomy. "Autonomy" is a much friendlier word, a less pompous word, than "independence."

Sint Maarteners or Saint Martiners need not because of some difficult turn they must make forget the days when the well was dry or almost dry, the days before Juliana Airport and the American tourists. Now that life is somewhat better (for some of us), we must learn to be modest, to *cool it*, to cherish old relationships, to be creative in suggesting new relations with old friends and family, and to work towards their conceptualization and implementation.

Notwithstanding the dismal role it played in the slave trade along with other European nations, Holland has been and continues to be a country of tolerant, liberal-minded people. The life experience and the writings of the great Spinoza attest to this reality. The Dutch understand that there can come a time when a relationship must change in order that special ties and long friendship remain. They understand that there is no life without change.

The language of instruction in public schools everywhere is always linked to the official language of the land. The official language, the language in which justice speaks is almost always the language of the people. There are still a few exceptions to this general rule, which is why I say "almost- always." Sint Maarten and Saint-Martin are two such exceptions.

The language-of-instruction issue is a constitutional issue of the greatest importance. As such, it should be considered in the context of a constitution that is conceived and written for a people whose official language is English. In this land, such a constitution is still non-existent, which is why the language of instruction issue is such a delicate, difficult problem.

English will not become the language of instruction in the public schools of St. Maarten by itself, without it being implemented. Implementation cannot "happen." To implement is to execute, to put in place, to do, to accomplish, etc. English as the language of instruction will have to be implemented—that is, put in place. One should not wait for something that cannot happen. One can try and make something happen.

# March 23, 1990

(*The Chronicle*, March 23, 1990)

To the memory of Élie Gibbs and Hervé Williams

It seems that March 23 is a very special day in the history of our Island. According to the Agreements of the Island of Saint Martin of March 23, 1648, it was on this date that the groundwork was laid for the physical partitioning of this island, a partitioning which was to follow the Treaty and that is still the subject of much debate, much controversy. It was on March 23, 1648 that the "Accords de l'Isle de Saint Martin" (Agreements of the Island of Saint Martin) were signed.

Having recently secured a copy of the original text or treaty, and after comparing this French text with the only two English translations of the treaty that I'm aware of, namely the translation done by A.H. Stronks, which appears in J. Hartog's "History of Sint Maarten and Saint Martin" (1981) and the translation which appeared recently in "St-Martin's Gazette, La gazette historique de Saint-Martin," both of which appear to be the work of persons whose native tongue is not English, I felt that it might be interesting, instructive and maybe even useful to attempt my own translation of this important document, and to submit it to "The Chronicle" for publication on this 23rd day of March 1990, along with my recently acquired copy of the official French text or treaty.

At the very least, my translation is more complete than Mr. Stronks', for if I'm not mistaken, his text does not include the first four lines of the original document or the last two lines, which are followed by seven signatures. It is important to note that Mr. Stronks did not translate from the original French text but from a copy of said original as this copy appears in Du Tertre's "Histoire des Antilles."

In his "History of Sint Maarten and Saint Martin," Dr. Hartog, referring to the partition treaty of 1648, writes: "In fact, Du Tertre's book is the only source from which we know the text." (Hartog, 1981: 36)

As for the very recent translation published in the *St-Martin's Gazette*, though we must always encourage all such efforts to shed light on our past, this translation is clearly the work of a person or persons whose native tongue is not English.

The publishing of this copy of the original *Agreements*, first in the *St-Martin's Gazette* and now in *The Chronicle* is an important step towards making this document, which was declared lost, more accessible, more available, to the general public and to researchers.

In the *St-Martin's Gazette*, we are informed that the original text or treaty is in the archives of *Aix-en-Provence* in France, and that a copy or double, dating back to the period in question, is located in the Treaty room of the *Quay d'Orsay* (French Foreign Office).

Several other interesting documents are published in the

*St-Martin's Gazette,* most of them for the first time. There are, for example, some reports written by A. Descoudrelles. Auguste Descoudrelles was the first Commander/Governor of French St. Martin who was not appointed by the Governor of Guadeloupe. Is that why he remained so long in St-Martin and did so much for the island? He was the first Governor appointed directly by the government in France under a new system in which the French government (in France) appointed the Commander/Governor of St. Martin and St. Barths. These two islands formed one district until 1784, when St. Barths became Swedish.

Descoudrelles was Commander/Governor from 1763 to 1785 (22 years), the first Commander to remain in office such a long time. It would appear from his writings and from the testimony of others that he was an exceptionally good administrator, an enlightened man, a visionary, who loved his country (France) and believed in the future of this island. Here is a statement found in one of his reports:

"...If St. Martin were a bigger, more important island, this pond (the Simpson Bay Lagoon) would be the prettiest and most favorable location that nature could have bestowed, because it would be very easy and not too costly to give this pond another communication with the sea."

Are the developers of Port de Plaisance inspired by Descoudrelles? Of course, given the century in which he lived, it is quite possible that this Frenchman loved the French side more than the Dutch side.

Thanks to his writings, we know that until 1772, article 8 of the 1648 treaty was not put into effect; the actual, physical partitioning did not occur. Moreover, his *Remarques* or *Comments* on the treaty of 1648 are an intelligent, informed and insightful reading/interpretation of the Treaty.

Like a master surgeon, Descoudrelles dissects the text. Nothing escapes him, especially not the title from which he astutely and, I believe, correctly infers and argues that by agreeing to the wording of said title, both Commanders claimed possession and governorship of the entire island of Saint Martin.

The various Descoudrelles reports of that period are aimed at convincing his government in France of the necessity of executing or implementing article 8 of the Treaty. It was during his governorship that the Count of Ennery, Governor of Guadeloupe, gave the Governor of Dutch Saint Martin six months to obtain authorization from Holland to implement article 8 of the Treaty. The six months came and went and so did the Count of Ennery, but it is surely Descoudrelles' steadfastness, his determination, which brought forth the implementation of article 8 of the treaty of 1648.

In his *History of Sint Maarten and Saint Martin*, Dr Hartog informs us that in 1772, Jan de Windt Jr. received orders to mark the boundaries of Sint Maarten. (Hartog: 40) The stone wall that a tractor made its way through in Bellevue a few days ago is, most likely, a section of the "slave wall" that was erected in compliance with said orders.

Life, like language that mimics it, is full of paradoxes: Auguste Descoudrelles, this great Governor who worked so hard for his country and for the "plantocracy" of French Saint Martin, whose care and welfare he was entrusted with, this great administrator, chronicler and visionary is also the man who is perhaps the most responsible for the partitioning of Saint Martin. He is perhaps the man the most responsible for causing a legal, a physical, line to be drawn across this land of one people.

Agreements of the Island of Saint Martin
of March 23, 1648 between the Commanders for the King of France
and the Commanders for the Dutch on the said Island

Today, March 23, 1648, have assembled Messrs Robert de Lonvilliers, Knight and Lord of Lonvilliers, Governor of the island of St. Martin for His Most Christian Majesty, and Martin Thomas, also Governor of said island for our Lord and Prince of Orange and the States of Holland and Henri de Lonvilliers, Master of Benevent; Savinier de Courpon, Master of Latour, lieutenant colonel on the said Island and David Coppin, lieutenant of a Dutch Company and Pieter van Zeushus, also lieutenant of a Company of the above-mentioned, who, on both sides, have agreed and hereby agree

Article 1:
That the French shall remain in the district where they are at present and shall inhabit the entire district that faces Anguilla.

Article 2:
That the Dutch shall have the district where the fort is located and the lands surrounding it on the south side

Article 3:
That the French and Dutch established on the said island, shall live as friends and allies together and shall not molest each other without it being a violation of the present treaty, which violation shall, therefore, be punishable by the laws of war

Article 4:
That if someone, be they French or Dutch,

is guilty of a crime or infringement of these agreements, or of refusing to obey the command of their superior, or of any other kind of offence, should withdraw into the other nation, the contracting parties bind themselves by these agreements to cause this person to be arrested and to be turned over to his Governor on the latter's initial request

Article 5:
That the hunting, the fishing, the rivers, ponds, fresh water, dyewood, mines or minerals, ports and natural harbors and other commodities of the said island shall be in common so as to meet the needs of the inhabitants

Article 6:
That French persons who are at present residing with the Dutch shall be allowed to side with and join the French, if they so desire, and to take with them their furniture, provisions and money and other implements provided they settle their debts or give sufficient guarantee, and the Dutch shall be able to do likewise on the same conditions

Article 7:
That if enemies should attack one district or the other, the said Masters, parties to this treaty agree that they must come to the aid and assistance of each other

Article 8:

That the boundaries and partitions of the said island which must be done between the two nations shall be submitted to His Lordship the General of the French and to His lordship the Governor of St. Eustatius and his deputies who shall be sent to visit the places and after they have made their report, they shall have their quarters delimited and shall proceed in the manner stipulated.

Article 9:

That the claims that might exist on either side shall be submitted to the King of France and the Gentlemen of His council and to His Lordship the Prince of Orange and the States of Holland. Neither of the above parties to these agreements shall fortify their position without contravening the said agreement and suffering all damages and interests in compensation to the other party.

Which was done and accepted on the day and year indicated here-above on a small hill nicknamed des accords, and the Gentlemen, parties to the agreements have signed in the presence of Bernard de la Fond, Lord and Master of L'Esperance, Lieutenant of a French company from St. Christopher.

Thus signed

De Lonvilliers - martin Thomas - H. De Lonvilliers - de Courpon - David Coppin - Pieter van Zeus-hus - L'Esperance.

# Mea Culpa – Yo Listenin t' Me?

(Part 1 of 2 parts)
(*The Chronicle*, April 4, 1990)

To the memory of Joseph Vliegen. For Maria Van Enckevort, Gerda Van der Kolk and all my former Colleagues at Milton Peters College

This piece was written in response to Mr. Wycliffe S. Smith's March 28th reaction to my *Syllogisms for a Dialogue?* Unfortunately, part 2 of my text could not be located. It appeared in *The Chronicle* on or about April 5, 1990. All efforts to locate it at the library in Philipsburg and elsewhere were fruitless.

> In themselves, all words are neutral or they ought to be, but we infuse them with our passions, and very quickly the passage from logic to a kind of epileptic seizure is consummated. That's how ideologies come into being; that's how they lead us into bloody farces.

So states, more or less, E.M. Cioran, the Romanian-born thinker who writes in blood and beautiful French. I see no reason to disagree with him.

Given Mr. Wycliffe S. Smith's March the 28th reaction to my *Syllogisms for a dialogue?* that appeared in *The Chronicle* on March 7th, 8th and 9th, given the tone of

Mr. Smith's discourse, it is obvious that I have failed to accomplish what I had attempted: try to underscore in a modest yet earnest way the all-pervasive role that language (the spoken-written word) plays in the lives of us human beings.

At this critical juncture of our story, of our history, I had hoped that by discussing what I regard as the language-justice connection or dialectics, I might have shed some glimmer of light on the importance of language in general and of a "language of instruction" in particular.

It is obvious that Mr. Smith felt offended by what I wrote or he would not have written, in reaction, that I was "arrogant" towards him and "insolent" towards Mr. Groeneveldt.

I would not reply to his reaction were he not an advisor to the Island's Executive Council on matters pertaining to education, and had he not misread my text to the degree I believe he did.

In any case, I trust that the Advisor has not advised, will not advise, my boss, Mr. Groeneveldt, to get rid of this impertinent, this *arrogant,* nay this *insolent,* teacher of French who hails not from Saba like Mr. Smith but from Saint Martin, and teaches in Sint Maarten.

In what I hope is simple English, here is the crux of Mr. Smith's argument as I understood it expressed in the speech he read on February 21, which appeared in *The Chronicle* on February 26. Here is what Mr. Smith stated and later wrote: *"If English is not made the language of instruction, English will become the language of instruction anyway."* (The italics are mine for emphasis.)

To this statement made by Mr. Smith, I countered, and I persist in countering, that, given the specific political-administrative-juridical (legal) context of Sint Maarten, English will not become the language of instruction, if persons do not plan and *deliberately make it* the language of instruction.

The entire thrust of my argument with reference to Mr. Smith's speech stemmed from and is centered on this oral and written statement/argument he made, and from which I thought might flow certain strategies for tackling the language of instruction issue, given Mr. Smith's position as advisor to the Executive Council.

In attempting to refute my above argument, Mr. Smith proceeds as follows: "I take it that Mr. Hunt does not believe in the last part of that sentence 'it will take place by default,' so let me omit this." That is like me saying or writing: "John is a nice person, but he is unreliable" and when someone reacts to the complete statement made, I then reply: "You are confused, arrogant and insolent. You should not have considered the part about John being unreliable. You should have considered only the first part of my sentence, the part about John being a nice person."

In my *Syllogisms for a Dialogue?*, I referred to Mr. Smith as follows: "Mr. Smith is obviously a very educated and talented individual, but he does not see the interconnections, the interrelationships -the dialectics of the problem. If he sees them, he has neglected to express them." In his reaction, Mr. Smith wrote that I am "arrogant and insolent, someone whose confused article elicits confrontation rather than dialogue."

Here is an example of my confused insolent arrogance. Here is how Mr. Smith attempts to refute my arguments: "He (Mr. Hunt) mentions that the panelists and the press should ensure that the various points of view expressed at such meetings are published. "Yet, I have not seen Mr. Hunt's philology of the language of justice and morality in any of the newspapers."

Let us take a close look at this statement. Let us dissect Mr. Smith's syllogism. Here is his argument:

Major (A): If Mr. Hunt's philology (speech) had appeared in one of the newspapers, I (Mr. Smith) would have seen it. Minor (B): I (Mr. Smith) have not seen Mr. Hunt's philology (speech) in any of the newspapers. Given A and B, therefore, Conclusion (C): Mr. Hunt's philology (speech) did not appear in any of the newspapers. Therefore, Mr. Hunt does not practice what he preaches, therefore ... etc, etc.

The problem with this argument is the weakness, the shakiness, (might we say the arrogance?) of the major premise. Mr. Hunt's speech could have appeared in one or both of the newspapers without Mr. Smith knowing, without him seeing it. That is precisely what occurred. The speech I read on February 21 appeared in *The Chronicle* on February 23. Mr. Smith did not see it; therefore, he did not read it. Is this an example of my confused, insolent arrogance?

# Fragments for Ruby Bute

(*The Chronicle*, April 20, 1990)

For Youmay Dormoy and Lasana M. Sekou

"When STRIFE had reached the lowest depth of the whirl, and LOVE was in the middle of the eddy, (under HER do all these things come together so as to be one, not all at once, but congregating each from different directions at their will). And as they came together, STRIFE began to move outwards to the circumference. Yet alternating with the things that were being mixed, many other things remained unmixed, all that STRIFE, still aloft, retained; for not yet had it altogether retired from them, blamelessly, to the outermost boundaries of the circle, but while some parts of it had gone forth, some still remained within. And in proportion as it was ever running forth outwards, so a gentle immortal stream of blameless LOVE was ever coming in …. And as these things mingled, countless tribes of mortal things were spread abroad, endowed with shapes of every kind, a wonder to behold."

—Empedocles (490-435 BC); (John Burnet's
1930 Rendition)

"These kinds of LOVE never drop dead. They are much too peaceful and mild. They honour you with a golden crown on your head."

—Ruby Bute; *Speak of Love*: p.40

If I had kept my sprat net, Ruby B., I would throw it far and high and wide on the LOVE in your words; on all that LOVE in your eyes, Ruby B.

Sitting in "Chez Max" with a friend Saturday afternoon eating "stew fish and red bean peas and rice," a young man looms up from the street, his eyes ablaze like a shaman who has tasted the rice of the dead. He is loud, almost aggressive. He greets my friend profusely and asks to be treated to a drink. He is restless. He walks away from our table and sits at the bar. There is no one there. He is talking aloud to us and to shadows we cannot see.

The young man: "Presents, man! Presents! If you see the presents I have for my mother. My mother loves me, my mother loves me.

My friend: "The girl will soon come back. You'll get your drink, but how are things with you, my friend?"

The young man: "Cool, man. Cool, real cool. I'm okay now, my mother loves me. Presents, man! You want to see presents?"

The girl has returned behind the bar. She serves him the drink.

The young man continues his monologue: "My mother... Presents!"

The girl: "Presents? What presents? Where would you get presents? You don't have any presents. What are you talking about? What presents?"

The young man swallows the drink and disappears into the street without saying goodbye.

> If I had kept my sprat net, Ruby B., I would
> have thrown it high and far and wide on the
> LOVE in his words; on all that LOVE in his
> eyes. If only I had kept my sprat net, Ruby B.

# All Aboard: An Open Letter to St. Martiners

(*The Chronicle*, March 12, 1992)

For Ambroise (Boisy) Halley, Alex Choisy and Louis (Loulou) Hyman

Marine biologists and my friend Roger Petit will confirm the fact that sprats live longer and better when they swim closer together. When sprats stick together, when they form a "thick bed," barracudas are fooled into believing that they are up against a mightier predator and the barracudas act accordingly. On March 22, 1992, St. Martiners must stick together; they must outmaneuver the barracudas.

My fellow St. Martiners, I could never succeed in conveying the immense, uplifting and overwhelming joy that came over me when I learned that, at last, at long last, St. Martiners had decided to come together and set sail together for their future, for the future of their children, for the future of St. Martin. "Together" is, of course, the key word here. This coming together is, indeed, an event of historical magnitude. All St. Martiners must embark on this historical journey. They must climb aboard this great ship of hope. They must support the "St. Martin List."

It took a lot of courage to bring forth a "St. Martin List." Those directly responsible for its existence should be commended, but more importantly, they need, they deserve, the support of all St. Martiners. St. Martiners must not let them down.

I am confident that if we stick together, we'll earn the respect of politicians in Guadeloupe and in France, who will have to listen more attentively when our elected representatives speak on our behalf.

A "St. Martin List," as opposed to a "Guadeloupe List," is of historical importance. It marks a turning point in the history of St. Martin. It signals a new politics, one that is no longer fuelled by bitter quarrels between families extending over generations but by a keen awareness, a realistic assessment, of the enormous stakes involved, of the difficult task which lies ahead of St. Martiners on their journey, in their effort, to survive as a people.

It is therefore absolutely necessary to unite, to combine forces, to climb aboard a single swift schooner in order to negotiate, in order to overcome, the storms ahead. Let there be no doubt at all, this journey will be hazardous. Gales and ground seas are awaiting us.

This decision to sail together, this coming together of St. Martiners for St. Martin, must have been painfully difficult for many. It took a lot of courage. It takes a lot of courage to set aside old differences, old animosities. It takes a lot of courage to set aside the infighting, the double-crossing, —the deadly crippling self-doubting that kept St. Martiners splintered, fractured, divided and vulnerable; a scattering of sprats that barracudas were feasting upon.

Thank heaven all of that is ebbing, receding, abating. At last, at long last, most St. Martiners have come to realize that while they were feuding, infighting and bloodletting, others were arriving, settling and consolidating. Most St. Martiners have come to realize that even though their roots run deep and strong in this tiny place called home, they are a people on a fast track towards political extinction. Most St. Martiners have awakened to the fact that their last ray of hope, their only chance of surviving as a people, is by overcoming, by uniting, by coming together, by transcending their petty differences, in order to avert a somewhat self-induced, self-inflicted political genocide.

Despite all of the above, St. Martiners must not overlook the very unfortunate fact that the names of some of the most able, experienced and dedicated St. Martiners are absent from this "St. Martin List." I'll spare you a list of names for fear that I might overlook someone. No matter the reason, no matter the circumstance which led to the absence of such able individuals form the list, all efforts must be made to enlist them for this journey, to include them on this voyage. All efforts must be made to solicit their adherence, to secure their allegiance. This is a unique opportunity. It may very well be the last chance for national reconciliation and for political survival as a people.

Three hundred and forty-four years ago, on March 23, 1648, "Agreements" were signed between representatives of France and Holland. Despite its shortcomings, this historic treaty goes a long way in underscoring our specificity, in testifying to the uniqueness, to the unique, complex nature of our political reality.

My fellow St. Martiners, 344 years later to the day (minus a day) on March 22, in a few days, we must rise up to the challenge we face. We must climb aboard this ship of hope. On March 22, 1992, we must vote for the future; we must vote for St. Martin and on March 23, on "St. Martin Day," we must celebrate our victory.

# Au bord de la Falaise des Oiseaux : Lettre ouverte au Père Charles

To the memory of Norbert Questel; for Adrien Questel and Maurice Cannegieter

Remis aux responsables du *St-Martin's Week* vers la fin-mars 2001, ce texte n'a pas été retenu pour publication.

« La destruction la plus radicale est celle qui s'en prend aux racines de l'être. »

Marcel G. de V. Placoly

Mon Père, vous qui savourez la langue de Molière aussi bien que vous possédez celle du grand Shakespeare, vous qui citez en latin les belles et généreuses paroles du Christ et des Pères de l'Église; vous qui aimez la bonne chère, les plus vieux cognacs, les bons vins de Bordeaux, la musique de Brahms; vous qui, comme moi et tant d'autres dans nos îles, avez si bien appris à vous fondre dans l'autre, à mimer vos maîtres, nos maîtres; vous qui persistez à vouloir nous civiliser via un micro du haut du Fort-Louis, comme si, comme si on ne vous avait pas limogé, renvoyé, destitué; vous, mon Père, dont la belle voix douce et grave coule comme une huile sacrée, étiez-vous dans le coup? Saviez-vous ce qu'on tramait?

J'ai un peu honte, Père Charles, de vous écrire sous le

couvert de l'anonymat, honte d'avouer ma crainte de nos petits maîtres. Ils n'aiment pas dialoguer, ils ne souffrent pas la contradiction, mais ils sont forts, mon Père. Ils règnent sur les hauteurs et dans les profondeurs. Ils sont souterrains. Le saviez-vous? Le savez-vous?

Non, mon Père, je ne pense pas être atteint de paranoïa. Ce mal-être me viendra sûrement si la vie dans notre île persiste à m'enlever tout espoir, toute espérance, tous mes amers. Ce mal me viendra sûrement si on s'obstine à me gommer la mémoire et mes lieux de mémoire, à me pousser encore et toujours plus loin dans la marge, loin, trop loin d'un centre où je trouvais jadis un équilibre dans l'ombre fraîche des flamboyants de Roland.

Mon Père, je me sens de plus en plus marginalisé, comme acculé à l'extrême, les pieds nus sur la pierre tranchante de la falaise des Oiseaux. J'ai honte de m'être reculé si docilement comme j'ai honte de ce texte anonyme que je commets. Pardonnez-moi ma couardise, mon Père.

Permettez cependant que je me présente à ma manière. À quelques exceptions près, je suis à l'image de notre peuple, du petit peuple saint-martinois; de ces gens que je cherche en vain dans les rues de Marigot, de Saint-James, de Colombier, de Grand-Case, de Quartier d'Orléans et des autres coins de notre île. Je suis à l'image de cette communauté noyautée, silencieuse, muette et en voie d'extinction. La douloureuse histoire de mon île, mêlée à celle de ma vie m'a rendue tel.

Notre communauté, la communauté saint-martinoise ne

Gérard M. Hunt

date pas des années soixante. Notre peuple a une Histoire pleine d'histoires. Il a sa mémoire collective et ses lieux de mémoire. Comme tous les êtres le moindrement équilibrés, nous avons un centre autour duquel nous nous sentons en équilibre comme à l'ombre des flamboyants de Roland. Nous avons un centre loin duquel le mal-être s'installe en nous, et nous perdons notre astre. C'est le désastre! Nous en sommes presque là, mon Père, là, à midi, en plein soleil, refoulés, confinés nu-pieds sur la pierre tranchante de la falaise des Oiseaux.

Père Charles, vous qui venez de Sainte-Lucie, qui avez œuvré si longtemps, si efficacement au sein de notre communauté pour combattre l'influence jugée pernicieuse de l'anglophonie du nord de notre île, étiez-vous dans le coup? Cette supposée maladie qui nous arrivait de l'Oncle Sam via le sud de notre île, saviez-vous qu'il fallait la combattre à tout prix? Le saviez-vous? Étiez-vous conscient que vous meniez là une lutte à mort, une sorte de Saint-Barthélemy? J'en doute, mon Père.

La « Ebenezer Methodist Church » a brûlé. Vous avez recueilli ses fidèles rue de l'Église. Quant à moi, je persiste à croire qu'on s'est servi de vous comme on s'est servi d'autres, comme on se sert de nombre de gens d'ici et d'ailleurs. Votre tâche étant considérée achevée ou votre profil étant devenu trop encombrant, on a jugé opportun de vous limoger via l'évêché. La République est laïque, mais la pieuvre a de très longs tentacules.

Voici, mon Père, quelques données, quelques lieux de mémoire que tout Saint-Martinois devrait savoir; or, vous êtes Saint-Martinois, mon Père, donc... Fin des années soixante, début des années soixante-dix, le constat est fait. Saint Martin, l'île de Robert de Longvilliers et de Martin Thomas, ces flibustiers-squatteurs par excellence, est à la dérive. **Soualiga** dont ils se sont emparés après le départ des Espagnols et par le truchement des « Accords ... de 1648 », dérive. Saint-Martin, le nord de l'île, perd son nord. Il devient de plus en plus noir, de plus en plus riche, de plus en plus anglophone, de plus en plus américanisé et protestant. Il s'engouffre dans l'anglophonie et le protestantisme, entraîné par l'américanisme venant du Sud et des alentours. Pour nos petits maîtres, ce café est trop noir. Il faut y ajouter du lait. Ce lait viendra de France. Quelques années plus tard, pour pallier cette injustice, nos petits maîtres en rajoutaient une: ils ouvraient large les vannes aux ressortissants étrangers de la Caraïbe et de partout ailleurs.

Voilà, Père Charles, le problème tel qu'appréhendé par nos petits maîtres de l'heure et sa solution telle qu'envisagée par ces messieurs. Le maire Hubert Petit y fait obstacle. Il faut, à tout prix, s'en défaire. Nos petits maîtres sont puissants. Ils « lèvent » l'obstacle. Le maire Petit est vilipendé. Il est persécuté, bafoué, humilié par nos petits maîtres et par une trop grande partie du peuple crédule. En 1976, il perd sa fonction et son titre. Divisez-les pour mieux les confondre, les soumettre et les contrôler; devise digne d'un Machiavel.

Rien n'a changé, mon Père, cette stratégie, vieille comme le monde, est bien vivante, ainsi qu'en témoignent le nombre des candidats aux Municipales ce mois de mars 2001, l'atmosphère générale de ces élections et les attaques *ad hominem*. Au lieu de s'unir pour la cause saint-martinoise, pour la cause du peuple, pour défendre notre communauté noyautée, on se bouscule, on s'invective, on se laisse aller à la violence verbale et physique, aux vieilles rengaines, au ressentiment, cette indigestion permanente qui sape les fondements de l'être. Au lieu de nous unir, de concentrer le peu de force qu'il nous reste afin de faire face aux petits maîtres de l'heure et à ceux nouvellement arrivés qui veulent nous mettre à leur pas, au lieu de canaliser nos forces, nos efforts, notre attention, nous nous dispersons, nous nous dissipons.

Mon Père, cette trop longue parenthèse risque de nous avoir écartés du sentier. Revenons-y. Revenons à nos petits maîtres et aux épreuves du maire Petit. Cet homme exceptionnel qui comme tout être avait ses faiblesses, ses défauts, ses partisans et ses détracteurs, ce fier républicain qui, à ce jour, bat pavillon tricolore, ce médecin doué et dévoué, ce Français de la Caraïbe, ce baroque Caribéen, ce Saint-Martinois de modeste famille, dont l'épouse venait de France, cet homme singulier est diffamé. Conspué et harcelé, il est rejeté dans la marge, loin du centre et de l'ombre fraîche des flamboyants de Roland.

Vous vous demandez peut-être ce que vous venez faire dans cette salade saint-martinoise, mon Père. Eh bien! La République est une, indivisible et laïque, mais à Saint-Martin, la religion du Père Labat agonisait. Le protestantisme (Méthodistes, Baptistes, Évangélistes...) gagnait du terrain. Saint-Martin était en état de perdition. Il fallait, de concert avec le blanchiment et la francisation, réanimer le catholicisme, il fallait le réadapter à la situation. Il fallait à nos petits maîtres de l'heure un Père Labat antillais. Voilà peut-être, mon Père, comment, pourquoi vos maîtres, de concert avec les nôtres, vous ont placé parmi nous.

Mais, il y avait des écueils insurmontables, mon Père. Premièrement, il fallait combattre l'anglophonie ambiante et l'influence de la culture américaine, tout en ménageant ces poules aux œufs d'or : les touristes américains. Deuxièmement, il fallait composer avec l'existence, avec les réalités du Sud de notre île, avec son dynamisme, son ouverture sur le monde et ses rapports avec les Américains en particulier. Il fallait composer avec le libéralisme de la partie néerlandaise de notre île, avec l'existence de l'aéroport Juliana et plus récemment avec le port par où entraient les nombreux touristes américains, voire des anglophones qui visitent l'île chaque année. Il fallait composer avec l'existence de cette frontière virtuelle et de cette anglophonie planétaire dynamique, hautement médiatisée, culturellement plus attrayante et plus proche du peuple autochtone saint-martinois que ne l'était, que ne l'est l'unilinguisme francophone ciblé par nos petits maîtres. Il fallait composer avec tous ces éléments sur lesquels nos petits maîtres n'avaient aucune emprise directe. Mais, comble d'ironie, à mesure que nos petits maîtres s'évertuent à franciser, à « hexagoner » le nord de notre île, le peuple autochtone saint-martinois, Nord et Sud confondus, s'enracine dans l'américanisme ambiant et dans l'anglophonie.

Troisièmement, et comme pour ajouter plus d'emphase

à cette scène déjà carnavalesque à l'extrême, la très grande majorité des nouveaux arrivés de France et de la francophonie s'est établie dans la restauration et dans l'hôtellerie. Cette majorité qui parle de plus en plus haut et fort a très vite compris qu'il fallait au moins ménager les poules aux œufs d'or, mais demandez au Saint-Martinois de souche et il vous dira que les « Métros » aiment le dollar, mais qu'ils détestent les Américains. « En effet, les Français haïssent les États-Unis...» écrit Jean-François Revel de l'Académie française, dans son dernier livre *La grande parade – essai sur la survie de l'utopie socialiste*. Selon Revel, cet antiaméricanisme est ancré dans une certaine haine du progrès et la peur du libéralisme. Les Saint-Martinois sont imbus de libéralisme.*

Les Saint-Martinois n'ont pas peur du progrès, mon Père. La manifestation de cet antiaméricanisme primaire – les apartés indiscrets, les commentaires désobligeants envers les touristes américains choquent les Saint-Martinois. Cet antiaméricanisme les dérange non seulement parce qu'il est néfaste au tourisme, à la survie économique de cette île, mais aussi parce qu'il est absurde, inepte et foncièrement injuste.

Le dernier écueil, le plus nocif, voire le plus explosif, le plus dangereux pour nous tous, mon Père, c'est l'écart, c'est le fossé, c'est la mésintelligence qui se sont creusés entre les populations nouvellement établies, la métropolitaine en particulier, et les Saint-Martinois autochtones, entre « les Métros » et les « Blacks », entre « the White Man » et « We ». On voit bien où tout cela pourrait nous mener, Père Charles.

Mon Père, il faut mettre un terme à cette trop longue lettre anonyme. Elle ne se veut ni jérémiade, ni appel aux barricades, ni incitation à l'invective, au ressentiment, au racisme, à l'exclusion, à la xénophobie; à la violence. Elle se veut une réflexion, une rétrospection, sorte d'anatomie, un modeste et trop long précis de décomposition de notre peuple, le peuple saint-martinois. Par-dessus tout, cette lettre anonyme se veut constructive.

Vous et moi, mon Père, et beaucoup d'autres dans cette île, savons ou devrions savoir que nous ne rétablirons pas facilement un équilibre souhaitable. Nous savons que de la Falaise des Oiseaux aux flamboyants de Roland, la route est intérieure dans tous les sens du mot. Nous savons qu'elle sera longue et douloureuse, mais qu'il faut sans tarder se mettre en marche. Nous savons que c'est par la parole, dans et par le dialogue que nous viendra une solution acceptable, honorable et durable au pressant dilemme que nous vivons. Vous et moi savons, mon Père, que la violence n'atteint presque jamais les puissants qui vivent sur les hauteurs au-dessus de la mêlée. Vous et moi savons que la violence atteint presque toujours les pauvres, les petits, les vieux, les faibles, les innocents, les laissés-pour-compte.

Voilà, mon Père, ce que j'avais à vous dire et, par ricochet, à dire à toutes celles, à tous ceux qui voudraient bien nous suivre de la Falaise des Oiseaux jusqu'à l'ombre fraîche des flamboyants de Roland.

*Environ six mois après la rédaction de ce texte où je faisais référence à l'antiaméricanisme français, les événements connus depuis sous l'appellation « 911 » ou

« Onze septembre » allaient plonger le monde dans une nouvelle ère, entraînant dans leur suite de sérieuses frictions politiques entre les États-Unis d'Amérique, la France et le monde entier.

Un an plus tard, le 11septembre 2002, P. Roger faisait paraître *L'Ennemi Américain : Généalogie de l'antiaméricanisme français* aux éditions du Seuil. Si ce livre avait paru quelques années plus tôt, Messieurs Chirac, de Villepin et autres décideurs français l'auraient sans doute lu et l'impasse absurde, regrettable et tragique survenue au siège des Nations-Unies ne se serait *peut-être* pas produite. Tout comme l'Angleterre, l'Australie et nombre d'autres nations, la France aurait appuyé les États-Unis. Les autres puissances européennes auraient sûrement emboîté le pas. Face à de vraies Nations-Unies, Saddam Hussein, qui savait que son pays n'avait pas ces fameuses « armes de destruction massive », aurait, sans doute, cédé et consenti aux inspections réclamées par l'O.N.U. La guerre d'Irak n'aurait *peut-être* pas eu lieu.

# On the Edge of Bird Cliff: Open Letter to Father Charles

For Horace M. Whit and Léopold Baly

"The most radical destruction is the one that targets the core of one's being."

V. Placoly's M. Gonstran

This Open Letter appeared in *The Daily Herald* on March 29, 2001, with sufficient misprints to render it unreadable. It was signed "The Mongoose." I hope the text is more readable here. I also trust that Father Charles and his sympathizers will forgive any impertinence they may uncover in this letter, for there is none intended.

Father, you, who relishes the French language as much as you delightfully master your own; who quotes so well in Latin the early Fathers of the Church; who enjoys a good meal, great old cognac, the best French wine and classical music; you, who like so many of us, have learned so well to mirror your masters, our masters—were you in on their scheme?

Father, you, who persists in trying to educate us, to civilize us by way of a microphone perched on the Fort Hill, as if they had not dismissed you, as if they had not discharged you, as if they had not fired you—were you privy to their plan? You, Father Charles, whose soft, sturdy sweet voice flows forth like some strange sacred oil—did you, know? Did you know what you were doing?

I am somewhat ashamed, Father. I'm ashamed of addressing you under the cloak of anonymity, of having to hide like a mongoose, but that is the only way the poor beast has survived thus far. I am ashamed of having to acknowledge openly my fear of the masters, our little masters. They are not open to dialogue, cannot stand being contradicted, but hey are powerful. They reign high above and deep down below us. They are underground and all around. Did you know that? Do you know that, Father?

No, Father Charles, I don't believe that I'm paranoid, but if they persist in rubbing out all that I aspire to—all of my plans, my hopes, my dreams—soon that illness will surely strike me. That sickness will surely come my way if they persist in erasing my past, if they succeed in doing away with all my seamarks, all the mooring of my heart. That illness will no doubt strike me if they keep pushing me further and further towards the edge, away from the center, where, once upon a time not so long ago, I used to feel secure, at home in the shade of Roland's Red Trees.

Father, every day, I feel more and more cornered, pushed back and away from the hub, driven further and further towards the edge where I now stand barefooted in the scorching sun on the sharp and pointed rocks of Bird Cliff. I am as ashamed of having backed away quietly as I am of writing you this anonymous letter. You must forgive me this cowardly act, Father.

Still, allow me to introduce myself the best I can, given the circumstances. Allowing for some minor exceptions, I am the image of our people, the little people of St. Martin, of those people I keep looking for in vain in the streets of Marigot, of St. James, of Grand Case, of Colombier, of French Quarter and the other parts of this island. I am the image of this community that is being overrun, a people who are muted, speechless, running scared and very close to extinction.

My community, the St. Martin community, does not date back to the 1960s. Our people have a history full of histories, full of stories. It has its collective memory. There are no cathedrals, but there are hills and valleys, gutters and old trees. We have no annals, but we have the sand, the sun and the sea that have witnessed everything. They have witnessed the spoliation, the injustice. They have seen the red men, the white men, the black men, and all the women. They have witnessed their commingling. They have seen everything! We have chewed up all of that, we have chewed up all of them and we have swallowed everything.

We claim each and every one of them. We claim all their commingling. We claim everything. That is our strength. But as with all fairly well-balanced human beings, we have a hub, a center close to which we feel secure, at home, like in the breeze under Roland's Red Trees. We have a center far from which we begin to lose our bearing. Life becomes unbearable. We are almost already there, Father, at high noon, in the scorching sun, barefooted, confined and cornered on the hot sharp-edged rocks of Bird Cliff.

Father Charles, you, who hails from St. Lucia, who have worked so long, so effectively, in this community to stave off the influence of the English language, did you know what you were doing? Protestantism, this presumed black plague that the Great Satan Uncle Sam was sending our way via the South of this island—did you know that it had to be checked? Did you know that? Were you conscious that you were involved in a struggle, in a subtle sort of Saint Bartholomew? I doubt it, Father.

The Ebenezer Methodist Church burned down. You welcomed its congregation into the Catholic Church. I persist in thinking that they have used you as they have used a number of other persons from here and abroad. Having deemed your task completed or your acquired profile too imposing, they decided to get rid of you via the bishopric. The Republic is secular, but it is a giant octopus with far-reaching tentacles.

Here are a few facts, a few trail markers that French St. Martiners ought to know: End of the 1960s, beginning of the 1970s, a survey is completed. It concludes that Saint Martin, the fiefdom of Robert de Longvilliers and Martin Thomas, those buccaneering-squatters par excellence, is adrift. **Soualiga** that they occupied after the departure of the Spanish, and by means of the "Agreements ... of 1648," is drifting.

French Saint Martin, Saint-Martin, is losing its compass. It is becoming richer, blacker, more Anglophone and more Protestant. Saint-Martin is going adrift. Driven by the "Americanization" of the southern side, it is sinking into the English tongue and the Protestant faith. This coffee is much too black. Some milk must be added. This milk will fly in from sweet France. A few years later, to make up for this injustice, our little masters will add another one: they will open the floodgates to foreigners from the Caribbean and elsewhere.

There it is, Father Charles! There is the problem as our masters assessed it and its solution as they conceived it. Implementation soon revealed that Mayor Hubert Petit was an obstacle that had to be overcome at all costs. Our masters are powerful. In 1976, they "did away" with the obstacle. And this most gifted St.-Martiner was vilified, persecuted and ridiculed. He was forced out of office by our little masters, assisted by too many of our people.

Divide and conquer. That is the motto of those true disciples of Machiavelli. Nothing has changed, Father Charles. The strategy, as old as the world, remains the same. Witness the number of candidates for the municipal election this month of March 2001. Witness the personal attacks, the overall atmosphere of this election. Instead of coming together to defend the cause of St.-Martiners, we rehash old gripes, we lapse into resentment. Instead of assembling, of concentrating the little strength we have remaining, in order to stand firm against our little masters; instead of channelling all our efforts and attention, we are dispersing our energy, dissipating our strength.

Father, this much-too-long digression may have taken us off the trail we were traveling. Let us return to it, to our little masters and to the ordeal of Mayor Petit. Like all human beings, the Mayor had his weaknesses, his faults. He had his supporters and his detractors. This proud French Republican, who, to this date, flies the French flag over his residence, is also a gifted physician, a son of the soil, a man of modest origin. This Frenchman of the Caribbean, this St.-Martiner was nevertheless defamed, hounded, persecuted. He was driven out of office.

Father, by now you may be asking yourself where you fit into this imbroglio. Well, the Republic is one, indivisible and professedly secular, but in French Saint Martin, Father Labat's religion was dying. Protestantism (Methodists, Baptists, Evangelists,) was gaining ground. French Saint-Martin was in a state of inequity, of depravation. Catholicism had to revitalized and tailored to the situation. Our masters were in need of a Father Labat who was West Indian. Maybe that is why your "Church masters," in concert with our "State masters," decided to place you among us?

There were several insurmountable obstacles to this undertaking. To begin with, the so-called "pernicious influence of American culture," and specifically the prominence of English in French Saint Martin, had to be dealt with. But this had to be done while allowing the hens to lay their golden eggs. In other words, the hens could lay but they must not cackle. Secondly, our masters had to come to terms with the existence, the realities, of Dutch Saint Martin, with its dynamism and its relations with the Americans in particular. They had to deal with its liberalism. They had to come to terms with the existence of Juliana Airport, over which they had no control whatsoever and, more recently, with the deep-water port through which the American tourists, all of them Anglophones, enter the island.

Our masters also had to come to terms with the existence of a border that is virtual and with a language (English) that is dynamic, international, highly mediatized, culturally attractive and closer to the native St. Martiner than the French unilingualism; the targeted objective of our masters. Our little masters had to deal with all these elements over which they had very little direct control. Ironically, the more they attempted to frenchify the northern part of the island, the more the native French St. Martiners continued to speak English at home and among themselves.

Thirdly, and as if to add more spice to this already extremely spicy stew , the vast majority of the new arrivals (from France and from the French-speaking world,) established themselves in the hotel and restaurant business. This majority that speaks louder and louder every day understood very quickly that they had to be careful in dealing with the hens that lay the golden eggs, but ask any native Saint Martiner and they will tell you that the "Metropolitans" love the dollar but despise Americans. "The French hate the United States…" writes J.F. Revel of the "Académie française" in his latest book titled *The Great Parade: Essay on the Survival of the Socialist Utopia.* According to Revel, this anti-Americanism is rooted in a certain "hatred of progress and in the fear of liberalism." St.-Martiners are not afraid of progress. St.-Martiners are steeped in liberalism. The manifestation of this primitive form of anti-Americanism, the negative remarks concerning

American visitors, disturbs the native St.-Martiners. This anti-Americanism is disturbing to them, not only because it is harmful to tourism, the economic survival of this island, but also because it is absurd, inept, primitive and unjust.*

The last obstacle, the most noxious, the most harmful, and the most threatening to us all, Father Charles, is the divide, the gap, the chasm, the profound misunderstanding that has developed between the newly arrived populations (the "Metropolitans" in particular) and the native French Saint Martiners; between "les Blacks" and "les Métros," between "We" and "The White Man." One can easily see where all of this could lead us.

Father, I must put an end to this much-too-long anonymous letter. It is neither whining nor a call to arms, neither incitement to invective nor to resentment of any kind. This letter is not an appeal to racism, xenophobia or violence of any kind. It is foremost a retrospection, a sort of anatomy, a modest and too-long account of the decomposition of our people, the native Saint Martiners.

Father Charles, you and I, and many others on this island, know, or should know, that bringing about a desired equilibrium will not be easy. We know that from the sharp-edged rocks of Bird Cliff to the sweet shade of Roland's Flame Trees, the road is interior in all the meanings of the term. We know that this road is long and painful, and that we must start walking right away. We know that dialogue is the only viable path towards an honorable solution to the pressing dilemma that confronts us. You and I know that violence almost never reaches the strong and the powerful, for they live high above the fray. You and I know that violence almost always strikes the poor, the old, the weak and the innocent. That is what I had to tell you, Father, and through you, tell all of those who would care to walk with us from the edge of Bird Cliff to the soft sweet shade of Roland's Flame Trees.

*Roughly six months after the publication of this "Open Letter" in which I referred to French anti-Americanism, the events known today as 911 moved the world into a new era and in its aftermath brought forth much friction between the U.S.A. and France. One year later, in September 2002, Philippe Roger's *L'Ennemi Américain: Généalogie de l'antiaméricanisme français* [later translated as *The American Enemy –The History of French Anti-Americanism* (2005)] came off the presses in France.

I believe that if this book had been published a few years earlier and read by Messieurs Chirac, De Villepin and other French leaders, the events which led to the American invasion of Iraq after 911 might have been managed differently at the United Nations. There might not have been a war in Iraq, for France might have closed ranks with the U.S.A. and Great Britain. Other nations may have followed suit, forcing Saddam Hussein to back down and allow all inspections to go forward.

# American Bashing at *Les Infos*

*(The Daily Herald,* October 8, 2001)

For Jules (John) Tondu

If, among the few Americans remaining on the island recently, there was one who could read French and who, perchance, picked up the magazine *Les Infos* (No. 204, September 21), here is what he/she would have read in the editorial. Here is what this American visitor to our shores would have been treated to in French:

"It is neither democracy nor the West that was attacked on September 11, it was the United States. The distinction is fundamental even if the suspected enemies of the Americans share none of the values which are dear to us.

"Never in history has there been a nation so universally despised as are the United States of America.

"Hundreds of millions of Arabs, of South Americans, of Asians and of Africans drink Coca-Cola, enjoy American movies and music, dress in Nike. Still they consider the Americans as the predators of the planet.

"By wanting to govern the world unilaterally, and in keeping with their sole economic interests, they have built an immense capital of resentment directed towards them, resentment they had superbly ignored until this attack. With an unbearable arrogance so typically American and a unilateralism in dealing with all nations and all groups that do not follow the road mapped out by the stars and stripes, it is no surprise that during the last few decades so many volunteers have stepped forward to combat this country which, outside of its borders, doesn't seem to respect any of the principles it now invites us to defend, now that it is wounded within for the first time since Pearl Harbor.

"If indeed it is bin Laden's men or his shadowy followers who transformed Manhattan into a mass graveyard, these men were trained in Afghanistan and Pakistan, in camps which were installed, financed and equipped by the American government that was ready to use anyone to combat the Russian presence in Afghanistan. This is how we got bin Laden and a regime in Pakistan that is deeply implicated in the Islamic extremist movement."

Let us now take a close look at this editorial. Let us begin with the last and main argument of the editorialist of *Les Infos*. This argument is, of course, a perfect *non sequitur*, that is, it does not necessarily follow. (A) The Americans helped the Taliban to fight off the invading Russians. (B) Seven years or so later, after having driven out the Russians, the Taliban turned on their own people and began persecuting them.

Because (A) precedes (B), it does not necessarily follow that (A) *caused* (B). In other words, because Marc took up drinking after his wife Paca left him, it does not necessarily follow that it is Paca's departure that caused Marc to start drinking. Marc and Paca could have remained together, and still Marc could have turned to drinking.

The editorialist of *Les Infos* is either a sophist or he does not know what a *non sequitur* is. Moreover, he seems to find it quite logical that so many countries and persons are resentful towards the U.S.A. and its citizens.

Our American visitor, who most likely would have come to our friendly shores in search of sand, sea, sun and maybe some cigars, would have remained "pantois," that is, flabbergasted by the overall tone of this editorial, whose only redeeming feature is the distinction it tries to establish, albeit clumsily, between the Muslim faith, the Arabic world, and the fanatics.

The entire editorial is an exercise in America-bashing, the kind of thing that springs forth from what some French intellectuals refer to as "l'antiaméricanisme primaire," primary in the sense of purely irrational, unfounded and uncontrolled.

The message that the average reader of French gets from this editorial is that the Americans and/or their government brought these attacks upon themselves, that they reaped what they had sowed, that the bully had been bullied. This editorial reeks of resentment, a resentment that seems to gush forth from the mind of the editorialist and commingles with the resentment of all those he cites in his editorial. It is a resentment that pours forth in ink that soils page 5 of *Les Infos*.

Americans, towards whom St-Martiners have always been friendly, must not be confused by this editorial. They must not be confused concerning the way St-Martiners on both sides of this friendly island felt on September 11, 2001, concerning the way we shall continue to feel towards the U.S.A. and its citizens.

# A Fantasy of Feathers?

*(The Daily Herald*, December 24, 2001)

For Lee Halley and Élie Williams

French cocks cannot sing *cock-a-doodle do*, no matter how hard they try. Listen to cocks crow in French St. Martin! Listen well, and you'll hear: *Cocorico! Cocorico!*

Early in the morning, long before the sun breaks the horizon, the spangle gamecock shakes the dew from his plumage then wings it down. Below, *cocorico!* He struts about, wings low, his crest ablaze, and paces nervously, anxiously.

He is waiting. He is awaiting each and every hen that hits the ground. He is a master at "treading down." He treads each hen and treads them all with the same intensity, the same vitality, the same arrogant authority... *Cocorico! Cocorico!*

Somehow I feel that one of the deep-rooted dreams of many of us male St. Martiners—and indeed of many male West Indians—is pure fantasy, a fantasy of feathers; a desire *to have* a mighty, magnificent, majestic cock; a yearning *to be* a superb, splendid, strong spangle cock...a *gamecock*, of course!

The *gory-cock* is definitely not a bird we fancy being. The gory is a born loser. No one identifies with a loser. No one wants to be a loser. The gory-cock is an abject creature. His gores point to his impotence at battle. It is the signature of a loser. When the going gets rough and bloody, the gored gory-cock will turn tail and run. The spangle gamecock, on the other hand, will fight to exhaustion or death.

There is something in the gory "sport" of cockfighting that answers to some call-of-the-wild in us, something which connects us with some aspects, some part of our primitive past, some ancestral obsession, some fascination with blood and blood letting, some well-anchored mysterious connection with ceremony and sacrifice.

The "cock pit" is a sort of altar arena. Spectators assemble to participate in the celebration of this obscure yet sacred ritual wherein birds, partially plucked and thoroughly pampered, are fitted with needlepoint spurs of steel or shell. The cocks are eager to fight. A healthy, true-blooded gamecock will never cow, never refuse a fight. Pity the cock-fighter whose gamecock calls it quits, whose pampered bird decides to run or, worst of all, fly away from the pit.

The pit judge is a high priest and the handlers are his acolytes. Sometimes when a cock is gored in the head or elsewhere and the two birds are immobilized in the pit, some handling is allowed. The handlers leave their corner. They carefully unhook the spur from the rooster that is gored, then return to their "corner" of the circular arena.

Some years ago, when I was a boy, the rules allowed more handling on such occasions. I remember the first time I attended a cockfight. I think it was somewhere in St. James, but at least two old-timers have assured me that it must have been in the Marigot area. I don't recall how I gained entrance to the pit, but I remember that it was off limits to boys of my age.

I remember that I was seated not far from an American couple. As I recall, during one of the handling pauses, suddenly all of the attention moved from the handler in the pit to the stands not far from me. The American lady had fainted and had to be carried out by her companion and others.

I recall asking what was wrong with the lady, and someone explaining that it was "the blood, the spitting." One of the handlers, whose rooster had been gored in the head, had sucked the blood from the wounded head of his bird and spat it out in his corner of the pit not far from the lady.

Strange the way images, scents, savours and sounds trigger recollection. Strange, indeed, the way the mind selects its scenes, stores them away so deeply and retrieves them so quickly, so mysteriously sometimes. Say "cockfight," and sometimes I see the pit and a handler sucking the wounded head of his rooster and spitting blood, a lady being carried out and a boy all confused and curious, wondering why— almost always in that order.

# The Great Satan?

(*The Daily Herald*, December 28, 2001)

For John Piper and Gabriel Piper

Some of us who impatiently awaited the reaction of *Le Monde diplomatique* to the September 11 massacres were not at all surprised. Over the past several years since the Berlin Wall came tumbling down, this monthly newspaper has become the mouthpiece of those who believe in the existence of a "grand complot," a great plot.

According to this scenario, the U.S. and its "vassals" are imposing on the world a system (global/single-market-economy capitalism) that is unjust, to say the very least. The industrial nations are thus guilty of what the intellectuals who pen the articles in *Le Monde diplomatique* call *la pensée unique*: unique or single-minded thinking. They argue, or rather, they assert, that the developing nations of the world are victims of this one-track thinking. France, England and the other industrial nations are "lackeys" at the service of the Great Satan, the U.S.A.

Wherever there is a problem in the world, the Great Satan has caused it to occur. Those who disagree with this way of apprehending complex issues in an increasingly dangerously complex world, those who beg to differ with this form of paranoia, are considered sick, stricken with the disease of *la pensée unique* or excessive drive towards a single-market world economy.

Mr. Ignacio Ramonet, the editor of *Le Monde diplomatique*, sets the tone of the reaction to the September 11 massacres. *L'Adversaire* (The Opponent) is the title of his leading front-page editorial. When one labours through Mr. Ramonet's rhetoric, one discovers that the U.S.A. invented the U.S.S.R. in order to justify killing millions of communists all over the world, and the September 11, 1973 attack launched by the Chilean Air force on Allende's palace (La Moneda) is a "crime committed by the U.S. that matches the attacks on the Twin Towers."

We also learn that ever since the implosion of the U.S.S.R. in 1991, the U.S. has been without an opponent, without an alibi. Miraculously, "the September 11 attacks restored... the opponent!" Ramonet goes on to explain that now "radical Islamism" and "all enemies of globalization" risk becoming "the Opponent." The reactions in the other French media, including *Le Monde* and *Le Nouvel Observateur* (highly respected papers), are declared biased, in step with the Great Satan's grand plot.

"Unilateralism" and "King Commerce" are the general headings under which Mr. Ramonet summarizes the various articles in the more recent December 2001 issue of this monthly. On the last page of this edition (No. 573), there is a venomous, vitriolic article by an enraged writer and literary critic. The target of Ms. Pascale

Casanova's diatribe is none other than V.S. Naipaul, the Nobel Prize Laureate, whom she accuses of betraying, of repudiating, his origins. If we are to believe Ms. Casanova, Naipaul has repudiated his roots because he espouses the values of the West, admires Balzac, does not care for Joyce and has accepted a knighthood from the British. Ms. Casanova's conclusion is clearly laid out: Naipaul has no original talent; moreover, he has disowned his heritage, he has assimilated. He has repudiated his own people. For all of this, the Nobel Committee has awarded him its prestigious prize. Beyond these affirmations, her insinuations are obvious: awarding the Nobel Prize to Naipaul is part of the Great Satan's grand plot.

In fact, Naipaul, a native of Trinidad, the writer of Indian extraction who spent all of his adult life in England and on the road throughout the world, is accused of repudiating his roots because he has had the foresight and the courage—as great, sensitive, learned and gifted minds sometimes have— to express his views on various subjects, which, as it happens, throw a monkey wrench into the scenario of her "great plot."

It is, of course, ridiculous to assert without furnishing substantive proof that the author of *A House for Mr. Biswas, Miguel Street, The Enigma of Arrival* and other such great books is an alienated West Indian who has repudiated his roots. To try to buttress such assertions by quoting Derek Walcott and Salman Rushdie out of context is dishonest, to say the least.

Ms. Casanova's blunderbuss of blame strongly resembles, in tone and in thrust, the deprecating articles that appeared in the French "intellectual" left wing media in 1960-1961 after another West Indian-born personality had won the same Nobel Prize for literature. Then, they had accused Alexis Leger (pen name: Saint-John Perse) of having repudiated his French West Indian roots, and the Nobel Committee of being in collusion with the "Ugly Imperialistic – Capitalistic – Americans." *Praises! To sing a childhood*, a childhood spent in Guadeloupe, is the heading of a group of St. John Perse's poems.

Some might wonder why we should care about the ruptured rhetoric of Mr. Ramonet and associates. The answer is simple enough, I think. *Le Monde diplomatique* is the gospel of a great number of teachers, university professors and their students in France and abroad. One cannot help wondering why such otherwise highly educated individuals continue to fall prey to this particular form of paranoia.

Granted, globalization and unilateralism are of great concern. Granted, also, that Western industrial nations and the U.S.A. in particular have made serious mistakes. They have not always done what they should/could have done, but this world is not perfect, and complex issues need to be seen in some perspective. Therefore, the question* remains: what explains the persistence on the part of so many French intellectuals, of such a Manichaean apprehension of almost everything that is American?

   * Roughly one year after the publication of this article, my question was answered in Philippe Roger's *L'Ennemi Americain: Généalogie de l'Anti-Américanisme français,* a thoroughly researched and elegantly written book. English translation: *The American Enemy-The History of French Anti-Americanism,* University of Chicago Press, 2005- Translator: Sharon Bowman.

# Like a Frigate Bird: In Praise of Judge Brangé

(*The Daily Herald*, February 22, 2002)

For Mrs. Émilienne Brangé and Mr. Pierre Brangé

"Bernard Brangé is terribly sorry that they must announce to you his death which occurred February 11, 2002, in Saint-Martin, in the 76ᵗʰ year of his life…My wishes are that you not be sad for he has 'lived,' and he earnestly implores you to forgive him his absence, to bring tides of flowers, with no wreaths, and to speak in praise of him if you deem him worthy of it…Goodbye friends."

Thus read the "Last message of Judge Brangé" which appeared in the *St. Martin's Week* of February 12, 2002. (I've translated it from the French.) The message was signed "B.B." and it was flanked by a recent photograph of the judge sporting a shirt adorned with sailboats in the wind, sea birds in flight and the sun in the background.

Others, I'm sure, will praise the magistrate, the close friend, the loving father. I can only speak, in a modest way, of the lover of words and of the exceptional human being I've had the pleasure and the privilege of speaking with on a few occasions.

The judge Brangé I knew was the essence of kindness, courtesy and generosity—the qualities of a noble soul, which lift it beyond itself and impel it to place its self-interests after that of others.

It is fitting and fair that we praise a man who held praising in such high esteem and who praised so many St. Martiners so magnificently.

Most of us practice deprecation. Most of us are master deprecators. Judge Brangé was our antithesis. He held praise and praising as the ultimate tribute that a human being can pay another.

Some day when a social history of modern St. Martin is written, Judge Brangé must be there among the prominent figures. I cannot think of a more interesting research project than a study of the rulings of this judge.

When I think of Judge Brangé, I hear a long, long sentence without pauses, forever flowing, as if someone is reading Proust aloud. When I think of the man, I see a man-o-war bird far up in the sky. He is flying away from the calm, comforting center in search of *his* center, soaring higher, further, longer than all other sea birds.

When we read his last message closely, we see the master writer-humanist at work. The deceased is speaking to us, asking us not to be sad, for he has "lived." It's all in keeping with the style of the man who considered time (past-present-future) in all its complexity, a man full of sweetness and light.

Judge Brangé implores us to forgive him his absence. In

*Gérard M. Hunt*

this context, I take that to mean both his absence from the gathering of his family and friends on the occasion of his death, and his absence from life with us.

I did not go to the funeral home. I had no flowers to take there, but I can't help being terribly sad, terribly sorry, that we must henceforth speak "of" Judge Brangé, that we can no longer speak "to" him.

Judge Brangé has taught us how to live and to love. Like a frigate bird that had flown too long, too far, too high, Judge Brangé came home and showed us how to die.

- 135 -

# No Future with the Socialists

(*The Daily Herald*, June 12, 2002)

For Louis (Loulou) Jeffry

St. Martin's geographic location, the island's remoteness from continental France and from Guadeloupe, its Franco-Dutch treaty of 1648, its tourist-based single economy, its symbiotic relationship with its Dutch counterpart, and its ingrained liberal heritage—all of these—place St. Martiners much closer to the republican liberal right in French politics than to the socialists, be they in France, Guadeloupe or Martinique.

The considerable number of settlers during the past twenty-five years or so from metropolitan France, neighboring islands and elsewhere has not altered this entrenched fundamental reality. On the contrary, it has buttressed it.

When/if St. Martin and St. Barths become a fifth district of Guadeloupe; when/if St. Martin and St. Barths obtain "special status," there may be very little or no future whatsoever on either one of these two islands for any political party that aligns itself with the socialists.

Realities dictated by France's key membership in the European Common Market, by global economics and by so-called "free market imperatives" are conspiring to marginalize French socialism at the expense of French republican liberalism.

In view of all of this, it becomes obvious that my friend Louis Mussington, whose devotion to politics (life in the city) must be admired and praised, has, unfortunately for him and for us, climbed aboard the wrong train: the socialist train. That train cannot take us where we want to go.

Moreover, though a St. Martiner, Mr. Mussington is not the candidate. He is the "substitute" to the candidate, a socialist candidate. This deputy would carry little or no weight whatsoever in a new non-"cohabitation"government. President Chirac, who is aware of our problems and was willing to act on our behalf, had his hands tied by the socialist government of Mr. Jospin. Let us hope that in the new government he will be able to act.

Given all of the above, and given the context into which the June 9 first round runoff places St. Martiners for the second round runoff of June 16, I see no alternative, no better choice, than to climb aboard the "Chaulet train" with the hope that it takes us where we want to go.

And so, my fellow St. Martiners, for whatever it is worth, my assessment of the situation is that we must vote. On June 16, we must climb aboard the "Chaulet train." We must vote massively for the candidate of the "Union for the Presidential Majority." We must vote for Mr. Philippe Chaulet.

# If you Live in Marigot

(*The Daily Herald*, July 30, 2002)

For Stephan Petit and Marjolein Roos

The French call them *sucriers* (sugar birds). I don't know what others call them. My guess is that they are either finches or sparrows of a sort. As far as I know, St. Martiners have always referred to them as "yellow breasts." Along with the majestic man-o'-war bird, they are, by far, my favorite feathered creatures.

Nothing is as soothing and sweet as the song of a yellow breast, but sometimes at night their song torments me. Sometimes, indeed, jumbies disturb my sleep. They keep reminding me of the days when I used to silence this sweet singing. Yes! As a boy in Sandy Ground I used to slay sugar birds with small, smooth stones I gathered on the sea shore and shot in my bonza: my sling-shot.

For the last two years or so, I've been feeding a solitary yellow breast, placing sugar and water in a corner of the stairway of my apartment. His visits are mostly early in the morning and late in the afternoon. He enters through the louvers, eats and drinks to his heart's content, defecates everywhere he lands and flies away. He acts as if I have nothing to do with the sugar and water he finds on the stairway. I must hide in order to observe him, for he absolutely does not tolerate my presence.

I say "he," but he could very well be a "she." I doubt it, though, for this bird is too ungrateful. Only males are so thankless, so selfish. Never a song and he is always alone. He has never once during all these months brought along a friend to visit and dine. I have never ever heard him sing. Every day, each time he visits, he must go to great lengths to see to it that no other yellow breast, no other bird, follows him to and through the louvers.

I must vacate these premises, which will remain empty for some time. I'll leave him enough of an opening in the louvers, a full saucer of brown sugar and lots of water. I don't know how far this will take him. I imagine the letdown I will cause him when he has eaten all the sugar and drunk all his water. I see him persisting, returning to the empty sugarless, waterless apartment, and even though he has always shunned me, I can already sense the disappointment I shall cause him.

If you reside in Marigot and happen to see my feathered friend flying to and from the iron balcony, try and befriend him. Be kind to him. Feed him brown sugar, leave him water and expect nothing but his droppings in return. If you live in Marigot, do this for me so that the *jumbies* may let up on me.

# Will this Truck Get by the Barking?

*(The Daily Herald*, November 20, 2002)

For Aline Choisy

During the last two weeks or so, those of us who understand French and Creole, and who spend some time trying to keep informed, have been privy to the simulation of a debate on the dismal state of tourism in the French Caribbean, and in Guadeloupe particularly. I say "simulation" because in a debate there must be dialogue, a more or less rationale exchange of ideas, of points of view. Here, in this simulation, it is like listening to dogs barking at a truck passing.

The truck, as I see it, is the impulsion emanating from the present French government in Paris to try to give liberal democratic Capitalism a real chance within the Republic. The barking noise continues to be made by *some* union leaders and their members, most of them young anti-Capitalists, Socialists, Marxists, Green men and Green women, whose violence and rhetoric betray mindsets that seem devoid of consciousness, mindsets that are fundamentally, violently Manichean.

There is an old Arabian proverb that can be rendered in English as follows: The dogs are barking. The caravan is passing. In other words, the barking is incidental to the passing and vice versa; there is no significant connection between the *passing* and the *barking.* Therefore, one might reason: let the dogs bark, the caravan will go by them. This statement might be universally valid, except in the French Caribbean.

In these islands, we cannot assume that this new French, republican, capitalist truck will make it past the barking. We must, therefore, rephrase our syllogism into a question: The dogs are barking. Will this truck get by them?

The author (second from right) as a "Scout de France"

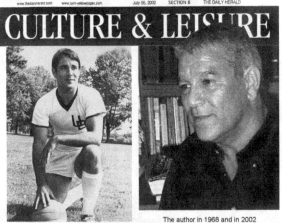

The author in 1963, 1968 and 2002

# A Short Drive to Denmark?

(*The Daily Herald*, November 30, 2002)

For Max Choisy and for Steve (Taco) Tackling

Among the statements reported by *The Daily Herald* to have been made at the *CaribNews* Multi-National Conference of November 7–10, 2002, the one that pricked me the sharpest into reaction was the statement reportedly made by Mrs. Sarah Wescott-Williams: "We have to ensure that there is a consistent link between St. Maarten and the U.S." (*The D.H.* of 23-11-02)

I take it for granted that the leader of the government of St. Maarten was referring to the lifeline, the vital economic link, which exists between the U.S. and St. Maarten, and to the flow-over onto the French side of this island. By lifeline, I mean our North American visitors with their U.S. dollars and everything else that flows from this reality. As Mrs. Wescott-Williams timidly intimates, without these tourists, Dutch St. Maarten, Saba, Statia, all of the Netherlands Antilles, all of this part of America (indeed, all of the Caribbean) would most likely resemble any number of mainland Guadeloupe communes—a process, a reality, that notwithstanding all of the above, is well on its way.

I say Mrs. Wescott-Williams *intimates*, because the "link" in question, the St. Maarten-U.S. link, is too preponderant, too important, too vital, to be referred to in such timid terms as those used by Mrs. Wescott-Williams. Nevertheless, given the overall context, given the ideological atmosphere of the said conference, the leader of the government of St. Maarten should be commended despite the mildness of her statement.

Those of us who are not as yet completely alienated still understand that no matter how much we try to be European, we remain American, for we are permanently anchored in America. We know that no matter the progress in technology, in communication and marketing possibilities on the horizon, for better or for worse, we are in America and shall remain there.

Listening to some among us whose alienation is much further advanced than ours, one wonders when, someday soon, they'll start driving onto the beach in Grand-Case, over the rocks in Point Blanche, off the clay-colored cliffs in Cupecoy into the open sea on their way to Paris, Amsterdam and other parts of Europe.

As for the statement "The U.S. Government should organize this Conference, it's not a Black issue," a statement reportedly made by Member of Congress, Maxime Waters, I say: Let a U.S. official (no matter what U.S. party is in power) attempt to play, be it even a minor part in organizing such an event in the Caribbean, you'll hear the vociferating, the accusations, of meddling ensuing from all our Caribbean-Europeans.

It is unfortunate, but for whatever it is worth, I believe that our alienation, both French and Dutch, will continue in its course, for it appears that the Caribbean-Europeans have managed to convince the U.S. State Department that the Caribbean is not in America but in Europe. The Caribbean-Europeans have drawn a solid red line between the U.S.A. and the Caribbean. It is an *ideological line*. It is a line that our pusillanimous leaders throughout the Caribbean skirt but never cross. It's a line that is leading us into a sea of estrangement, an ocean of despair. It is a line that we must endeavor to erase, to rub out completely, lest some day soon, some Sunday morning, we'll all get up, wash up, dress up and assemble for a short drive to Denmark.

# Walking the Last Walk:
## Remembering *Miss Arlette*

(*The Daily Herald*, June 3, 2003)

For Ginette, Josette and Jacqueline Tondu and to the memory of Alain Tondu

Sitting in the Catholic Church in Marigot listening to the priest read from the Good Book over what remained of Miss Arlette after her spirit had left her body I couldn't recall the last time I had seen that many St. Martiners assembled. It's a pity that we only come together on such occasions, to walk last walks down to Perrinon's estate.

Sitting there in the church, I could barely contain my emotions as I tried in vain to recall precisely the last time I had seen Miss Arlette. Later, at the cemetery, I was able to focus more clearly. I had seen her, I recalled, way back when I had visited *Mam* Buddy. I remembered how frail she had seemed then, but most of all I recalled rediscovering, reconnecting, with her smile—a soft, special, sweet smile.

Miss Arlette was a kind and gentle soul; sweetness, softness and light "all rolled-up into one," as my mother might have said.

Others may have known her as Mme Tondu, but as far back as I can recall she has always been Miss Arlette—

Alain, Ginette, Josette, and Jackie's mother. Sitting there in the church, I couldn't help reminiscing, going back in time, to the late fifties, early sixties, to The Golden Star, the best football team on the island, the team that used to trash "The Speed" every time we played them. Well, almost every time.

We, "The Golden Stars," used to muster at Alain's, at Miss Arlette's place, near the football field. There, we planned our game, drank the lemonade Miss Arlette made us and pined for a smile from one of her strikingly beautiful daughters.

As I walked the last walk down the church alley, right onto *Rue de la République*, left onto *Liberté*, past the old *Gendarmerie*, the *École des garçons*, where Mr. Ligarius used to try to teach us, past the Methodist Chapel, the *Palais de Justice*, past Mr. Pierre Jone's place, Miss Toutoule's rhum shop and my mother's place, past Miss Toto's wooden fence, and finally right onto Perrinon's estate, I kept wondering how many times Miss Arlette had walked this same route. Whose casket did she follow the last time she walked this walk? What was she thinking then as she moved slowly, silently?

There is something about this ritual, about these funeral walks of ours, that jolts some of us back to the essentials of existence, to the question of being; of time that is passing as we are passing through time.

As I stood in the graveyard trying to restrain my emotions, listening to the thudded sound of earth landing in the hole on the casket I could not see, I kept focusing on the smile until the thumping sound of the dirt and the bright sunlit afternoon and the tears of loved ones assembled, until all of this became almost irrelevant as it faded and Miss Arlette was smiling gently as we drank her lemonade.

# An Exemplary act of Representation

(Speech delivered in Marigot on July 5, 2003)

To the memory of Martial Jeffry and for Antonio Jeffry

Good evening, Ladies and Gentlemen:

Mrs. Jeffry has asked me to say a few words in the context of this presentation of her book to the public on this side of the island. I take this as an honor and thank her for the esteem and the confidence she has placed in me.

My fellow St. Martiners, those of you who are familiar with my views and sympathies know the importance I ascribe to language, to the spoken-written word, to discussion, dialogue and debate in general, to the fundamental relationship between language and politics. By politics, I mean life in the *polis*, the city, the community.

There can be no real community without language, without communication, without the spoken/written word. Therein lays the importance of language, of interaction, of communication in general, of a people's mother tongue, and of a people's history in particular.

Most of us know that the question of the St. Martiners' mother tongue is a very sensitive subject, more so on this side of the island than on the other side, the South side.

It is sensitive because it is political and, therefore, crucially important.

Unfortunately but understandably, as soon as one touches upon this nerve, one runs the risk of being misunderstood and being labeled anti-French, anti-foreigner, i.e., a member of the "born-here" crowd, a trouble-maker, an *agent provocateur*, etc. I am none of those. At least, I do not wish to be any of those, except to say that I was born here, and on that matter, I have no lessons to take from anyone, particularly from those who were born elsewhere but who act as if I must roll over like a dying cockroach.

Fellow St. Martiners, if the old sandbox tree that stands in Marigot, the only one remaining on the waterfront, should fall tonight without anyone ever acknowledging its presence, this old tree, so generous with its shade, would fade out of memory. If no one ever records its existence, attests to its presence, its bounty, this old tree would soon fade away; it would sink into oblivion, into nothingness. It would cease to exist due to a lack of representation.

Representation is the key element here. Representation goes hand in hand with survival and democracy. Without representation, democracy cannot exist. Democracy is representative government. We elect people to represent us, to make us present in our absence.

We, the people, cannot all be there at City Hall in Marigot, in Guadeloupe and in Paris checking things out for ourselves and making our own decisions. This is not possible, so we elect people to act for us. They get a mandate from us; they are our representatives. They make us present in our absence. They "re-present" us. At least, that is what they are supposed to do in a democracy. That is how all of this is connected. That is why we cannot get out of politics, because we cannot get out of language, of interaction. We cannot get out of representation, lest we pay the consequences.

Therein lays the importance of information, of communication, newspapers, literature, books and history books in particular. History deals with the lives and the development of people. It is the record and analysis of past events. A community that does not record and analyze events is a community whose days are numbered. To be without a history is to be outside of time, to have no existence, no being, as in the verb form "to be," as in "They are no more," as in "They are deceased, they are extinct."

Mrs. Jeffry's book deals with the lives and development of St. Martiners. That is what her book is all about, what it represents. That is why it is crucially important, fundamentally important. That is why we must not only present this book, but we must celebrate its publication that now makes it available to every school child in St. Martin, in every home library in St. Martin, in the libraries of the world.

Here is what an eminent French historian, the late Georges Duby, member of the distinguished "Académie française," wrote in the preface to the *History of France- From its Origins to our Days*. Here is what he wrote:

In our collective memory, the history of France appears like a succession of events whose framework, as time passes, becomes less and less disconnected, more and more tightly knitted and complex. That is why the passages of this book are punctuated with dates in order to pinpoint the precise moments of certain political or military events. (Duby: 1995)

When you read and analyze Mrs. Jeffry's book, as you must, keep all of the above in mind. With *1963, a landmark year in St. Martin*, Mrs. Jeffry invites us to consider and acknowledge the fact that her community, our community, the St. Martin community, does not date back to the sixties. Her book bears witness to the fact that, like all people, our people have a history, one that is full of events, full of true stories, full of *our* stories. This book brings home the fact that, like all people, St. Martiners have a collective memory.

We have no cathedrals, but we have our hills and valleys, our gutters and old trees. We have no annals, but we have the sand, the sun and the sea. These three have seen all the injustice, all the spoliation, all the suffering. They have witnessed everything! They have seen the red men, the white men and the black men. They have seen all the women and all the commingling.

To date, most historians are men who too often neglect to underline the role, the key role, of women, of great-grandmothers, of grandmothers, of mothers, aunts, sisters, wives. This St. Martin historian does not neglect them. She does not place them in the margin, on the edge, away from the center where they rightfully belong.

*1963 A Landmark Year in St. Martin / 1963- Année charnière à St. Martin* is a determined valiant effort to make sure, to see to it, that the St. Martin community does not fade out of memory, that it does not fall into oblivion, into nothingness, outside of time, outside of history; that St. Martiners do not cease to exist due to a lack of representation.

This history, this book, this exemplary act of representation, is the ultimate tribute that an individual can pay his or her community. Therefore, St. Martiners should, St. Martiners shall, forever be grateful to their historian, to Mrs. Daniella Jeffry-Pilot.

I thank you for your patience.

# Présentation/ Représentation/ Célébration

(Discours prononcé à Marigot le 5 juillet 2003)

For Édouard (Eddy) Baly and Christian Baly. To the memory of Christiane Baly

Madame Jeffry, Mesdames, Mesdemoiselles, Messieurs, chers collègues, chers amis,

Je tiens à remercier Madame Jeffry de m'avoir fait l'honneur de m'inviter à dire quelques mots dans le contexte de cette présentation de son livre au public en partie française.

J'estime, pour ma part, que cette présentation est synonyme de célébration. En effet, nous sommes ici rassemblés pour célébrer la parution de *1963- A Landmark Year in St. Martin/ 1963 – Année charnière à St. Martin*. Il convient de souligner le titre et la facture bilingue de l'ouvrage comme nous les a légués l'auteur.

« Le St. Martin d'autrefois était un village insulaire caribéen aux liens très resserrés ... ». Voilà l'incipit, les premiers mots du texte, le commencement. Un village, donc, ou comme plus précisément l'auteur nous l'explique, « un réseau de villages du Nord au Sud ou si vous préférez du Sud au Nord. Deux capitales : Great Bay (prononcé Gritbay) et Marigot (prononcé Marigut). Deux langues officielles, le néerlandais et le français, mais une seule langue – ciment du peuple : l'anglais st.- martinois ».

Après un bref historique du vieux Saint-Martin, du Saint-Martin de 1848 à 1963, s'appuyant sur des sources sûres, des rubriques de faits divers et autres articles de l'unique journal de l'époque, quotidien rédigé en anglais en partie néerlandaise, l'auteur nous replonge dans ce début des années soixante, dans l'année 1963 en particulier.

Les habitants du vieux Saint-Martin étaient pauvres, nous explique Mme Jeffry, mais les relations sociales qu'ils ont développées entre eux pendant plus d'un siècle après l'abolition de l'esclavage étaient exceptionnelles, voire exemplaires.

En effet, [i]l y a quelques années, dire que les habitants de St. Martin étaient un seul peuple aurait été d'une grande banalité. Aujourd'hui, il faut le dire très fort pour convaincre certains, tant notre identité se trouve bousculée, peut-être même submergée par un développement effréné, certainement déraisonnable.

Notre peuplement a connu beaucoup d'aléas à ses débuts. Chassés par les envahisseurs anglais à plusieurs reprises, les Saint-Martinois ne se sont pas découragés et sont, à chaque fois, revenus sur cette île où cependant il n'y avait pas grand-chose à faire : petite agriculture qui ne pouvait intéresser que des particuliers, pas de grosse société colonisatrice. Ceci nous a donné un peuple tranquille et travailleur, le travailleur et son maître partageant les mêmes difficultés à vivre sur cette terre peu riche. Les liens d'amitié se sont vite créés. Notre île, connue aujourd'hui comme la 'friendly island' des Antilles, le doit au fait que les enfants de toutes les couches de la population ont fréquenté la même école, balayant ainsi tout complexe de supériorité chez les enfants des maîtres – propriétaires – terriens et tout sentiment d'infériorité chez les enfants de ceux qui ont péniblement remué la terre. Ceci nous permet aujourd'hui d'être fiers et accueillants car nous ne nous sentons pas inférieurs à ceux qui arrivent.

Cette population est la même des deux côtés de l'île. Pendant trois siècles, les mariages entre les familles habitant soit au Sud soit au Nord ont été très fréquents, ce qui nous a donné une île où les habitants ne diffèrent que dans la façon de tenir leur drapeau. Certains le tiennent avec les couleurs verticales, d'autres horizontales. Nous avons donc les mêmes gènes à cela près.

L'école n'a pas été le seul 'melting pot'. Il y a aussi l'obligation qu'avaient les jeunes de l'île d'aller travailler ailleurs, soit à St. Domingue, Cuba, Curaçao, Aruba ou aux États-Unis, où ils étaient dans les mêmes champs de canne ou les mêmes usines.

Rien, en effet, ne donne autant le sentiment d'appartenir à une même communauté que de se retrouver dans les mêmes quartiers à l'étranger à faire face aux mêmes problèmes et le soir ou le dimanche à se réunir pour se parler de son cher pays Saint Martin. Ceci a été le lot de plusieurs générations de Saint-Martinois, et ce, jusque dans les années cinquante.

Les habitants des deux zones ont toujours lutté ensemble pour se défendre contre tout danger venant de l'extérieur. Ils se sont toujours prêté main-forte comme ils se l'étaient promis dans le Concordat de partage de l'île, le traité des Accords de 1648. (Petit : Discours du 28 mars 1990)

Chers amis, les mots que je viens de vous lire, j'aimerais bien pouvoir me les approprier, vous dire qu'ils sont les miens. Hélas! Je n'ai fait que répéter des mots déjà dits, le début d'un discours; paroles prononcées à Sandy- Ground, il y a de cela 13 ans – un soir de mars, plus précisément le 28 mars 1990 – par Monsieur le Maire, l'ancien Maire de St. Martin, le Dr. Hubert Petit. J'ai eu l'honneur et le plaisir à l'époque de traduire ce beau discours. La version anglaise a paru dans un journal de la partie néerlandaise. Monsieur le Maire avait été invité à prendre la parole par la SMECO, la « Saint Martin Educational and Cultural Organization ».

À moins que je ne me trompe, vous chercherez en vain aujourd'hui le texte français, l'imprimé de cet important discours fait par cet homme qui fut le Maire de Saint-Martin pendant 18 ans, soit de 1959 à 1977.

Chers amis, lisez *1963, année charnière à St. Martin*, l'ouvrage de Mme Jeffry. Comparez sa parole à celle du Maire Petit, et vous verrez qu'ils tiennent, tous deux, essentiellement le même discours. C'est qu'ils se sont abreuvés à la même source, celle de la mémoire collective st. martinoise.

Dans un récent ouvrage ayant pour titre *Sur l'histoire*, l'éminent historien français Krystof Pomian nous explique :

> (...) il est vrai, et plus que jamais, que l'histoire ne se fait qu'avec des sources. Mais nous savons aujourd'hui que, loin de se limiter aux seules sources écrites, l'ensemble des sources historiques est virtuellement illimité. Tout objet matériel, qu'il soit minéral ou organique, qu'il soit une production naturelle ou un artéfact – tout objet matériel peut être une source historique à condition de lui poser des questions auxquelles il peut répondre et de maîtriser les techniques susceptibles de le faire parler. (Pomian, 1999 : 381)

*1963, année charnière à Saint-Martin*, cet événement que nous célébrons ce soir, ce petit livre, quel questionnement provoque-t-il? Quelles questions lui poser? Comment faire parler ce livre? Comment l'écouter?

Prenez une feuille vierge, sur cette feuille blanche, tirez un trait soit à la verticale, soit à l'horizontale, divisant la feuille de manière à ce que vous ayez deux colonnes, une pour le Nord de notre île, l'autre pour le Sud, et dressez, là, l'inventaire des journaux de 1959 à ce jour. Certes, vous ne trouverez pas tous les éléments de réponse dans l'ouvrage de Mme Jeffry, mais son livre vous incitera à aller voir plus loin et ailleurs.

Cet exercice, vous l'aurez deviné, je l'ai fait pour vous, et voici ce que j'ai découvert, en voici le résultat : pour le sud de l'île, partie néerlandaise, de 1959 à ce jour de juillet 2003 :

1. *The Windward Island's Opinion*
2. *Newday*
3. *The Chronicle*
4. *The Guardian*
5. *The Herald*
6. *Today*

Six! Six journaux, chacun ayant existé pendant au moins quelques années. Les deux derniers, vous les connaissez. Six journaux sans compter divers pamphlets et autres feuilles ronéotypées.

Pour le nord de l'île, pour la partie française, la feuille est restée vierge. Certes, il y a eu les efforts louables de Mme Jeffry, de son frère Antonio et d'autres, de notre ami Baly Léopold, des membres de la SMECO. Il y a aussi bien sûr, et depuis assez longtemps maintenant, le *St. Martin's Week*, publication gratuite qui nous renseigne à sa manière, c'est-à-dire dans les limites de ce que j'appellerai son statut, ses pouvoirs. Il y a également les plus récents : *Our News, Fax Info, Côté News* et *Today Français*, mais à toute fin pratique, la feuille reste vierge. Pas un journal. Je doute que cette virginité soit synonyme de pureté, d'innocence. Cette blancheur dénote plutôt l'obscurité la plus totale, la plus débilitante. Soyons clairs. Je dis bien : aucun journal. Pas un seul journal.

Vous ne me croyez pas? Allez donc voir au mot « journal » ce qu'en dit le *Robert* de la langue française. Vous y trouverez une bonne définition : « publication quotidienne consacrée à l'actualité ». Pendant que vous y êtes, voyez le contenu d'un journal. Vous lirez : « annonce, articles, bandes dessinées, bulletins, chroniques, courrier, écho, éditorial, entrefilet, faits divers, feuilletons, illustrations, interview, nécrologie, rubrique, publicité, réclame ... » Vous en conviendrez, j'en suis certain, que la publicité, que les réclames font partie d'un journal, d'un vrai journal, mais que les réclames ne constituent pas, en elles-mêmes, un journal.

Chers amis, comment doit-on jauger la valeur, l'importance de l'événement que nous célébrons ce soir? C'est à partir du contexte que nous venons d'évoquer. C'est à partir de cet ensemble de circonstances qu'il conviendrait de mesurer l'ampleur de l'événement que nous fêtons ce soir, à savoir la parution de cet ouvrage, de ce livre sur notre histoire dont l'auteur n'est nulle autre qu'une des nôtres, la très grande, la très sage fille de Monsieur et Madame Jeffry, notre amie Mme Daniella Jeffry-Pilot.

Mes chers amis, le constat brutal, l'état présent lamentable que je viens de nous dresser ne doit aucunement nous inciter à chercher des boucs émissaires, notamment celles et ceux plus ou moins nouvellement arrivés parmi nous, comme étant responsables de la triste, de l'intolérable, de la dangereuse réalité dans laquelle nous vivotons tous.

Si, pour calmer nos démons, si, pour répondre à quelque appel primitif qui nous habiterait, il nous faut absolument désigner des coupables, ce sont nous-mêmes qu'il conviendrait d'élire. Par nous-mêmes, entendons, non pas le petit peuple saint- martinois qui n'a pas, qui n'a jamais eu, ni les moyens, ni le savoir-faire, la compétence, ni le loisir indispensables à l'épreuve en question, mais l'élite, les dirigeants, les responsables locaux et de passage, les plus ou moins lettrés et mieux nantis, celles et ceux qui, contrairement à Mme Jeffry, aux anciens membres de la SMECO et à quelques autres, n'ont pas cru bon s'investir dans un dialogue soutenu, conséquent, voire salutaire, ni entre eux, ni avec les autorités compétentes , ni avec les aïeux, avec la mémoire collective saint-martinoise.

Cela dit, à quoi bon, chers amis, sombrer dans une sorte de nostalgie revendicative, revancharde et rétrograde? À quoi bon nous complaire dans le ressentiment, cette indigestion permanente qui sape les fondements mêmes de l'être et qui débouche, presque toujours, dans la haine de l'autre, dans le manichéisme, dans la violence verbale et physique?

Prenons plutôt acte de nos erreurs, de notre errance dans cette longue nuit noire de 1959 à l'événement que nous célébrons ce soir, et à l'avènement d'un nouveau statut politique. Prenons plutôt acte de tout ce temps perdu et mettons-nous en marche vers l'avenir. La route s'annonce forcément douloureuse et longue. Il faut donc, sans tarder, que nous suivions le bel exemple de Mme Jeffry.

Mes chers amis, c'est par la parole et l'écriture, par la parole-écriture, par le dialogue et dans l'action responsable et raisonnée que nous viendra une solution acceptable, honorable et durable au présent dilemme que nous vivons.

Chers amis, ici assemblés, célébrons donc la parution de l'ouvrage de Mme Jeffry, ce flambeau qui nous rassemble, ici ce soir, et qui, vous le voyez bien, commence déjà à éclairer l'obscurité qui nous enveloppe.

Aux parents ici présents, il est toujours bon de rappeler, de répéter les belles et sages paroles du grand poète français, que voici : « L'ignorance est la nuit où commence l'abîme. Alors, aux petits enfants, donnez le petit livre. Marchez la lampe en main pour qu'ils puissent vous suivre ».

Je vous remercie de votre immense patience.

# This Train:
## Open Letter to St. Martiners

*(The Daily Herald,* October 31, 2003)

To the Memory of my Friend Berno Champare; of Roy Rogers and of all the other young promising St. Martiners who died tragically in December, 1972. Unless I am mistaken, this airplane accident, this disaster is nowhere listed, except in the hearts of parents and friends.

This train, the "Status Train," the one that is due on December 7 in this year of our Lord 2003, is *our train.* This is a locomotive that was conceived, designed and built for us. It's the kind of train we've been dreaming of all these years, one that can take us where we wish to go, where we need to be. This is a train we cannot afford to miss, one on which we must all embark.

I say this train was built for us, but you and I know quite well that St. Martin and St. Martiners are not that important that the present government in Paris—or any other French government—would offer us, and to us alone, the opportunity to secure a new status, one better suited to our aspirations.

In fact, this offer of "some autonomy" through a new status is extended to all communities within the French Republic. It is an undertaking that is dictated by other imperatives and to a large extent by France's membership in the European Community. It so happens that this opportunity or offer is a sort of ready-made suit that is exactly our size, exactly our fit, as if it was made for us. This offer is, therefore, somewhat providential, and it is an opportunity of historical importance.

But as promising as it is, this train is not equipped with arms that will reach out to us wherever we may be on December 7, 2003 and pull us on board. No! We'll have to cast our vote. If there are enough of us traveling, this train will get us where we wish to be taken. If there are too few of us, too few votes, St. Martiners will have no more excuses, no one to blame but themselves.

We shall no longer be able to blame the French government and even less our local politicians, for they will all have done their part. Indeed, for once in the history of modern politics in St. Martin, all parties are together, in agreement. For once there is unity in pursuit of a crucial objective: Securing a mandate for acquiring a new status within the framework of Article 74 of the French constitution.

It is only after parliament has approved the negotiated (new) regime by enacting it into law that election of the Deliberating Assembly of St. Martin can take place. At this juncture, we can be certain that party line politics will resume for the good of us all, as sure as the sun will continue to shine on St. Martin.

And so my fellow St. Martiners, for whatever it's worth, my humble opinion is that we have nothing to lose and everything to gain by riding this train, by voting to secure a mandate to acquire a new status within the confines of Article 74 of the French Constitution. However, on such an important occasion as this, it is good to bear in mind that it is with us voters as it is with horses, for as our old-timers might remind us: "You can get up for-day morning, take the horses to the well, strain yourself all day long pulling up buckets of water till the trough is running over, but you can't force the horses to drink."

# We Must Break Down
## the Old Walls

For Louis Hamlet and Julie Hamlet and to the memory of Jean-Luc Hamlet

Speech delivered on December 5, 2003, in Marigot. Due to time constraint, part of this text was omitted upon delivery.

Good evening, Ladies and Gentlemen! Bonsoir Mesdames, Mesdemoiselles et Messieurs! Ladies and Gentlemen, St.-Martiners of good will! Yes! We are of good will, by that I mean that deep down inside, each one of us would like to do what is best for St. Martin and for St.-Martiners. To do what is best for St. Martiners is to do what is best for St.-Martin, and vice versa. It is as simple as that.

But we St.-Martiners have been for too long a period in a sort of mental prison, a mental mould that has been constraining us, holding us back, dividing us, crippling our nature which is that of a gifted people, open to differences, to others, a friendly people, a proud and industrious people.

My friend François Petit is dead right when he states that the French Constitution of 1958 had locked out all possibility of statutory evolution for us, but we St.-

Martiners have also locked ourselves behind massive old walls of disunity and feuding. We have spent too much time quarrelling among ourselves.

The time has come, at last, when St.-Martiners have no alternative but to unite. Do or die. That is where we stand today. We have been in our mental prison too long. It is time that we break down the old walls, time that we let in some fresh air.

Chers compatriotes, concitoyens de notre vieille, grande République, il y a dans la vie de chaque être des moments où il faut absolument s'investir, des projets auxquels on ne peut se soustraire, des questions auxquelles il faut absolument répondre.

Mes chers amis, nos maîtres à l'ancienne école communale sur le front de mer nous ont inculqué des valeurs républicaines qui, pour ma part, m'ont toujours aidé dans ma vie d'homme, à l'étranger et dans notre île. Monsieur Ligarius et Monsieur Jean, tous les deux Guadeloupéens, seraient fiers de nous à cette étape, si...si le temps et la mort qui rongent tout avaient épargné nos vieux maîtres.

Yes, ladies and gentlemen, the question that our government has put to us is one such question we cannot refuse to answer. To refuse answering, to abstain from voting is to answer "No," and to answer "No" is to negate, to rub out forever all hope, all aspiration, the little that still remains of our culture, of our dreams, of our destiny as a people. Now is not the time for "No." It's time that we break down the old walls! It's time that we let in some fresh air!

My fellow St.-Martiners, we must be honest with ourselves and accept our failures. We must concede that we are a sorry bunch of resentful procrastinators and complainers. Like most St.-Martiners, I love big words. To procrastinate is to delay, to put off until later, until tomorrow. Tomorrow becomes next week, and next week becomes next month, and next month runs into next year, and next year never materializes, it never comes.

We St.-Martiners are also master deprecators, (another big word!) We enjoy belittling, putting down, denigrating other St.-Martiners. It's easier to tear down than to build up, so much easier to belittle than to praise. We have no confidence in our fellow St.-Martiner, in our sister St.-Martiner. We feel, and we act this way because we lack self-confidence. St.-Martiners will not encourage a deserving St.-Martiner. On the contrary, we go to great lengths to put him or her down – but we heap mountains of praise on others. We bend way down in reverence to perfect strangers. They come from all corners of the earth to tell us what is best for us, and we have more confidence in them than we have in our own people.

We St.-Martiners are also full of nostalgia. We like to reminisce the old days. Most people are nostalgic, but our nostalgia is laced with a deadly dose of paranoia and resentment. It is full of suspicion and distrust. We think everyone is out to get us. We love reminiscing, going back in time, remembering the wrongs that other St.-Martiners have done to us and to our great grand parents. We dream of settling old scores, of getting even.

Such behaviour, such resentment is like going by Enox and drinking five glasses of full cream milk, eating five *johnny-cakes*, and then some *bull-foot-soup*, all of this for lunch, every day of the week! I have no trouble with Enox making a dollar or two, but this behavior leads to a permanent indigestion. Resentment is crippling us as individuals, as a community, as a people. It's a sickness of the spirit, a sickness onto death.

Ladies and Gentlemen, St.-Martiners of good will! On December 7, 2003, on Sunday, the last train of opportunity will come our way and we'll have a chance, at last, to begin putting all this resentment, all of this belly aching behind us. We will have a chance to begin to force our destiny. We must not fail to climb aboard this train. We must have confidence in ourselves.

But, if after all of this preaching, you still have no trust in this St.-Martiner, listen to what a top-ranked French civil servant had to say about the importance and the urgency of St.-Martiners acquiring a new status. Let me read you how Mr. Fabien Giraud summarized the situation in 1998:

> Tout a déjà été écrit ou dit à propos de l'indispensable et urgente évolution statutaire de la partie française de l'île. Le temps n'est plus à l'indécision, ni aux vaines querelles; il est à l'action. L'heure est venue pour St. Martin de forcer son destin. (Giraud, 2002: Préface)

There is no way that I will step down from this podium without referring to the valiant work done by my friend Daniella Jeffry, without reading her translation of this passage. Here is the passage in English:

> Everything has already been said concerning
> the necessary and urgent statutory evolution
> of the French part of the island. It is no longer
> time for indecision or vain quarrels, it is time
> for action. The time has come for St. Martin
> to force its destiny.

St.-Martiners of good will, that is why, on December 7, we must tear down the old walls! We must let in some fresh air! We must force our destiny! We must vote YES for a New Status.

# In Praise of the Wild Mongoose

(*The Daily Herald*, February 14, 2004)

For Henry Brookson and Jules (Julo) Choisy

There are so many things that I could be doing right now, that maybe I should be doing now, rather than writing in response to Mr. Joseph Rudy Brooks' Mongoose Menace (*The Daily Herald:* 03-02-04). But I fear that his opinion might remain unchallenged, that no one might take time, precious time, to speak on behalf of, in praise of a dumb innocent, wild little creature.

It saddens me to learn that the mongoose is considered nothing but "a pest that should definitely be eradicated." There is no equivocation, no hesitation whatsoever. The mongoose "is a menace to the natural habitat," writes Mr. Brooks in complete agreement, so he states, with his friend Andy Caballero.

It surprises me to hear that "the local folks had a deep hatred for the mongoose," and it distresses me to discover that "ramming a piece of steel in the animal through a chicken wire cage seems to be the execution of choice lately."

Mr. Brooks failed to offer us a single valid argument, one sound reason to support his war on the mongoose; his declaration that the mongoose should be eradicated. Surely the fact that Mr. Brooks found a mongoose in his car eating his fried chicken is not convincing. I'm sure the mongoose did not realize that the car or the chicken in it belonged to Mr. Brooks.

Had the mongoose taken his time to think things through that day in 1994, he definitely would have selected some other car to climb into and somebody else's fried chicken to feast on. I'm certain that the mongoose didn't mean to offend, to "stun" Mr. Brooks the way he did. So why take the incident so personally, so seriously?

I strongly, empathically, disagree with Mr. Brooks and his friend. Not only do I believe that the mongoose should not be eradicated, I earnestly believe that the little animal should, at the very least, be protected from the barbaric cruelty of some of us human beings.

The mongoose is part of our cultural heritage. He is one of the very few animals present in our folklore. What the fox symbolizes in European and some other cultures, the mongoose represents in ours.

Old-timers trapped the mongoose where and when the animal competed with them for food—mainly eggs and chicks (or is it chicks and eggs?). Such commodities were scarce and, therefore, precious in those days; much more precious to them than they are to us today.

Granted that there were also some old-timers who used to pour kerosene on the trapped animal and use the little beast as a rapid mobile torch for setting fire to their huge grass-pieces. But how many old-timers owned estates with such grass-pieces to be set afire yearly? Old timers trapped the mongoose and some of them were very cruel towards the animal, but to my knowledge they never sought, never thought of, eradicating the little beast.

Old-timers admired the mongoose. For them and for many of us today, there is no animal as cunning as the mongoose. He is foxier than the fox. Swift and slick, he is the elusive prince of our underbrush, the little that still remains. Above all, he is ingenious and furtive. When cornered, he'll fight dogs, cats and Neanderthals to the very end. Those are traits most of us value, characteristics most old-timers admired. Maybe that's why when sick and delirious some old timers see him. "Look! Look! You see the mongoose?"

Maybe that's why old-timers sing his exploits; why, when revelling, they speak to him in lyrics and in rhythm— "Mongoose went in the mistress kitchen, take up one of her big fat chickens, wild mongoose! Wild mongoose, the dogs know your name! Wild mongoose, your name is far abroad!"—as if they are warning him, not threatening him; as if they are aiding and abetting him; as if they understand his plight; as if they are on his side; as if, like some of us old-timers, they are rooting for him.

# Unbridled Horse: Jumbies in Saba?

(*The Daily Herald*, May 28, 2004)

For Senator Will Johnson

Is India shining? Looking back on this great old civilization—today the largest, the biggest democracy on earth—who can deny its intellectual, moral, religious and political contribution? Who would wish to deny the enormous progress India has made since independence, particularly in the last twelve years or so?

India indeed is the world's largest democracy, and India is number one on the short list of places I would visit, if only... But India's obvious shining is not the issue. The point at issue here is Mr. Will Johnson's wild horse, his unbridled, runaway rhetoric; the dark side in his *India Shining* (*The Daily Herald*, May 19, 2004), i.e., his obvious pleasure, his delight, in stoning the U.S.A. while showering India with petals, as if his praising of India is but a pretext for bashing the U.S.A. and venting resentment.

I've not had the honor and the pleasure of meeting Mr. Johnson, but I've read some of his published writings and I admire the man who speaks his mind and values dialogue and matters of the intellect in this land (the Caribbean), particularly on this island where money talks so loudly that it deafens. I regret to say that I hardly recognized the author of *For the Love of St. Maarten* in this binary, this Manichean opinion entitled *India Shining*; in this regrettable oversimplification of fundamentally complex and important issues.

I have, therefore, concluded that some of the *jumbies* that have let up on me recently have crossed over onto Saba where they have set about bothering Mr. Johnson.

Mr. Johnson begins by telling us how elated he felt about the general political state of affairs in India and the outcome of the recent elections there. Then comes his first slam-bang: "The ruling Hindu nationalist party has been defeated by an *Italian housewife.*" That's the slam. Now the bang: "That would be the equivalent of a woman from one of the smaller Caribbean islands beating President Bush." (The italics are my emphasis.)

Never mind the strange shakiness of the simile. Let's consider Mr. Johnson's major premise, the foundation upon which he builds his arguments to get to his conclusion. Let's take a close look at the premise: "The ruling Hindu nationalist party has been defeated by *an Italian housewife.*"

The facts, in some context, are: Mrs. Sonia Gandhi (who was born in Italy of Italian descent and is the widow of former Prime Minister of India, Rajiv Gandhi, who was assassinated in 1991) has been living in India since 1968 (36 years!). She has been an Indian citizen since 1983 (21 years!). She speaks fluent Hindi (so what if she has an accent?) and she considers herself Indian.

In spite of all of the above, Mr. Johnson refers to Mrs.

Gandhi as "an Italian housewife." Despite his stated regard for democratic values, throughout his text, Mr. Johnson identifies Mrs. Gandhi by presumed otherness, supposed foreignness. Mrs. Gandhi is *"an Italian housewife;"* she is *"this Italian lady;"* the *"Italian woman;"* an *"Italian Roman Catholic."*

Such representation of Mrs. Gandhi contradicts Mr. Johnson's professed inclusiveness. It betrays a mindset that could place Mr. Johnson in the camp of those Indian political opponents of Mrs. Gandhi who belaboured and decried her presumed otherness. Reportedly it is precisely such representation of Mrs. Gandhi that impelled her to decline becoming the Prime Minister of India.

Mr. Johnson's *India Shining* is replete with such rhetoric, such representation that obfuscates complex issues instead of elucidating them. Such rhetorical representation permits him to arrive at a spectacular conclusion. Here it is in its entirety:

"India indeed is now shining as the world's greatest democracy, *whereas darkness induced by capitalist greed, and specifically by the rootless wandering commercial classes, permeates and obscures so-called democracy in the U.S.A.*"

The first part of his conclusion, *the slam*, is clearly stated, but *the bang*, (in my italics), that completes and renders his conclusion intelligible, has to be inferred from the various digressions and citations in his text.

Notwithstanding this rather severe reading of Mr.

Johnson's *India Shining*, I do respect his right to his opinion. I also believe that his heart is in the right place. For whatever it is worth, he remains one of my heroes. As for those island hopping jumbies, I pray they leave Saba and Mr. Johnson soon and that they do not return to St. Martin to resume bothering me.

# My Father's Hands

(*The Daily Herald*, June 19, 2004)

To the memory of my sister Christiane

My father stands at the dining room table, washing his hands in a white enamel basin. He is rubbing one hand in the other intensely, repeatedly, alternating as if there is some stain he is removing, some foul scent he is suppressing. It is night. I am outside in the almond tree, looking down and in at him through a window.

I am twelve years old or so. I am scared, but I am curious. He must not see or hear me, or heaven knows how long I will have to remain here aloft. The white enamel basin shines in the light from the kerosene lamp. What is on my father's hands that he spends so much time scrubbing them? He is rubbing one hand with the other and the white soapsuds contrast with his dark arms and hands. My father has beautiful hands; everyone remarks that my father's hands are beautiful.

My father is an awkward, angry man. He has no patience at all. He drinks, gets drunk, comes home late at night or early in the morning. Gawky, loud, aggressive and abusive, he roughs up my mother. She never knows what to expect. She is afraid. We are afraid of him. She runs away when she hears him, when she sees him coming. She hides at the neighbour's or in the treed grass piece behind our house, and she drags all of us along—two of my sisters and me.

That's what happened tonight. We are waiting for him to leave. When he has finished scrubbing his hands, after he has eaten whatever he has found, he will exit the back door into the yard, beneath the almond tree. He will shout ugly, nasty words. He will call my mother names, and then he will leave, swaying, reeling and rolling like a vessel in choppy weather, and we will not see him or hear from him again until the next time that he is drunken, angry and hungry.

It is night in 1955 or 1956. I am perched in an almond tree looking down at my father as he washes his hands, looking down at my mother and my sisters. They are waiting, all of them, crouched in Mr. Hanna's grass piece. My father is washing his hands in a white enamel basin, and the soapsuds are pretty on his dark hairy arms. That's one of the master scenes that flood my consciousness and start my heart pounding when the demons come drumming, insisting that I revisit the past, that I reconnect with my father.

They come in bunches, these scenes, one running into the other as if connected in the mind's eye by an invisible thread that seldom breaks. Thus, invariably, the frame moves from my father's hands in the light of the kerosene lamp to my mother's shadowy face late at night or early in the morning. I hear her voice as she shakes me out of my sleep. "Run! Run! You must run quickly up the street and fetch your uncle!" I must pound on the big gate and make sure that he gets the message. I must tell him to come right away. "He will understand. He will know why." My mother is frantic.

At this point, the screen always blurs, as if hundreds of frames are missing, forever lost; a gaping hole in my picture story. I must fill it in as best as I can. But no matter how hard I try, I can never remember running up the street. I can't recall that part at all. I don't remember delivering the message. My mother has assured me that I did. I don't remember. I just do not remember. I cannot remember. But I must have taken her message, for without failing, after the blurred segment, there is a scuffle, a fight; two men wrestling on a narrow balcony. One is thrown over its railing. It's my father. He lands on his back, gets up awkwardly and begins to climb back up the steps. Midway up, he turns around and gawkily climbs back down. He stands a few seconds against the balcony, a few seconds that always seem too long to me, then he starts walking away towards Miss Olive's Alley, skirting the wall of Mr. Pierre Jones' house as if he is searching for an opening between the old sandstones, looking for a breach large enough to penetrate. The last frame in my picture story, the last time I see my father. We had no photograph of him.

Like his mother before him, his sister (my aunt Edmée, once the prettiest woman in Grand Case), and his daughter, (my sister Christiane,) my father was afflicted with Huntington Chorea (Chorea, Latin for dance, from the Greek Khoros meaning "dance." Huntington Chorea, also called Huntington sickness or Huntington disease, is a nervous disorder.) The twitches, followed by the jerking, started when he was still a fairly young man. The dancing came later. But no one knew what was happening. No one was aware of the misfortune that was upon him, least of all my father himself.

The dreadful disease that to date remains without a cure, that had taken his mother, that was to take his sister and one of his daughters, was now upon him and he knew nothing— nothing other than life was a living hell, that his world was crumbling, that his life was going to hell. Like his mother and the others, like so many Huntington sufferers throughout the world, the illness twitched and jerked and then danced my father's life away into dementia onto death, away from St-Martin, in 1962.

Not long ago, I came upon my father on page 108 in Mr. Will Johnson's *For the Love of St. Maarten*, 1964 edition (Mr. Michel Deher's Collection). He was seated at the stern of a small fishing boat. He is seated across from his friend and fishing mate, Mr. Philibert Richardson (AKA Bèbère) who is blowing into a conch shell announcing the catch of the day. In the distant background, we see the old lighthouse at the foot of the Fort Hill. Behind the two men, across the centre of the 1952 black-and-white image, a wave is breaking upon the reef; a crest of foam, a swell of soapsuds. My father's arms and his left hand are clearly visible, at rest upon his thighs, at rest the way they were, the way they must have been, before the twitching and the compulsive nervousness began.

Now, when the demons come knocking, when they begin their drumming and the film starts rolling, I barely shudder. I see a wave breaking upon the reef, a crest of foam, a long swell of soapsuds. I see my father's arms at rest upon his thighs and his hands are beautiful, and still.

Author's Father in Left Corner of Photograph

Author's Mother (1984)

# Unequal Treatment: Adding Insult to Injury

*(The Daily Herald,* November 16, 2004)

For Omer Arrondell and Robert Weinum

The draft at issue here is not the drawing of a liquid, as from a cask or keg, nor the depth of a vessel's keel below the waterline. The draft at issue here is a rough sketch, a preliminary version of a document.

It is the *Avant-projet de loi organique et de loi (ordinaire)-Document de Travail* (the preliminary version of the fundamental set of laws designed to govern the new "Collectivity" of St. Martin – A Working Document).

When the people of St. Martin went to the polls on December 7, 2003 and voted for a new status within the French Republic, they did so on the basis of a pledge made to them by the State (France), more specifically by representatives of the present French Government, as well as by a majority of the local representatives of St. Martiners.

The promise made to St. Martiners was that their local representatives and the representatives of the State would negotiate a set of laws that would govern St. Martiners. I insist on the word "local," for the representatives of the State are also representing St. Martiners but from a different perspective—from the perspective of the State.

This draft is, therefore, a starter, the first written version of a set of laws destined to become the so-called "Organic Law" that would govern St. Martiners. This is a reality that St. Martiners had to expect and, in my view, accept, given the nature of the present relationship between the State (France) and its commune (St. Martin).

It was power politics that determined the mapping, the drafting of this first version of the Organic Law, both St. Martin's and St. Barths'. It is power politics that shall determine any redrafting, any major rewriting, of this initial version.

This first draft can be considered a sort of balloon by the State to gauge the political weather, to gather preliminary data in the political atmosphere. The representatives of the State will argue that it is St. Martin's fiscal deficit that impels the State to rein in St. Martiners, to restrain, to check them, while giving much freer rein to the citizens of St. Barths. This is adding injustice to injury, for it is the State (successive governments of France) that caused St. Martin to sink into its present fiscal deficit, a deficit that is now used by the State to justify unequal treatment under law.

Mayor Fleming has it right when he states that there is, here, a double standard, "deux poids, deux measures entre St. Barth et St. Martin." Indeed, a fiscal deficit does not exist in St. Barths, not because the people of St. Barths are the

better citizens than St. Martiners, but because the State could not do to St. Barths what it did to St. Martin: stand by and allow massive, savage, unbridled illegal immigration, thereby causing a fiscal-political deficit.

Mr. Victorin Lurel, the President of the Regional Council of Guadeloupe, a distinguished attorney, is dead right: "You must be reactive," he told the elected officials of St.Martin recently, "for the text of this draft is a regression... to the pre-1981 situation...We have here (in this draft) the image of a people who must be placed under guardianship, under trusteeship, of adults who must be kept on a leash." (*St. Martin's Week* – November 9, 2004 – my translation)

Mr. Omer Arrondell astutely points out that it is the State that is responsible for not enforcing the laws of the Republic, laws that would have kept St. Martin from sinking into fiscal deficit, a fiscal deficit that is inherently political and that is now used by the State to justify its lack of confidence in St. Martiners.

The double standard treatment referred to by Mayor Fleming must also be apprehended as a result of a geopolitical reality that is unique: the complex St. Martin/St. Maarten historical and geopolitical reality as this reality relates to France, the Netherlands, Europe and the Americas. I take this reality to be at the very heart of the matter. St.Martin's officials would do well to consult with St. Maarten's, and particularly with constitutional experts such as Mr. Ralph Richardson and Mr. Louis Duzanson before responding to the State on this matter.

Mr. Guillaume Arnell is reported to have stated that the elected representatives of St. Martin failed to "fill in all the blanks," contrary to the representatives of St. Barths, who "wrote" (their) own draft. I beg to differ with Mr. Arnell. The reality of the situation is that what the State (France) tolerated with respect to St. Barths, it did not allow for St. Martin. Therefore, St. Martiners should not reproach themselves or their representatives for failing where St. Barths has supposedly succeeded. Rather, it is more than time for St. Martiners to unite and remain united; time to make sure that their local representatives start haggling, bargaining. St.-Martiners should not accept unequal treatment under the law.

# He is Surely Rejoicing:
# Remembering Wilfred Trene

*(The Daily Herald,* January 25, 2005)

In Memory of Mrs. Maude Trene. For Mrs. Yvonne Gibbons and Mr.Maurice Trene

You may have never met my friend, the late Wilfred Trene, you may have known nothing of the man, but if you are curious, interested in living; in life that is so intimately linked to death, to dying, so inextricably connected that one is inconceivable without the other, …You may have never met my friend Trene, but if you had been present at his funeral service at the Methodist Church in Marigot on January 15, 2005, you would have witnessed a remarkable celebration, an exceptional event, an event that must not fall into oblivion for lack of representation.

Like most of us sinners, our friend Trene had his faults, his weaknesses, but at the core he was a decent, kind and caring man whose loyalty to family and friends was as strong as grape tree wood, as enduring as the pond side sticks, those mangrove shrubs with which he used to brace the wire of his fish pots in the sandy ground of his youth, the old Sandy Ground.

It is truly unfortunate, regrettable indeed, that the poignantly edifying, and elegantly delivered eulogy of the Reverend John Gibbons, Fred's nephew and caretaker, was not caught on film or, at the very least, recorded. Pity also those few who, though present for the service and in the slow procession to the graveyard, elected to remain outside of the church during the entire service and, in so doing, could not hear, see, witness or experience this event.

Had we caught it on film, the story of Fred's life as echoed in his nephew's eulogy would be the kind of warm, authentic material we could use in our churches and schools for the edification of our youth. Such pertinent, such eloquent, witnessing might speak better, louder, stronger to the minds and hearts of young St. Martiners than some of the cold extraneous programs of pedagogues.

I refer to Mr. Gibbons as Reverend Gibbons quite intentionally, quite deliberately. Though still not an ordained Minister of the Methodist Church, what John Gibbons has been doing for a considerable number of years is, indeed, nothing short of ministering. Long before his sojourn in England where he studied theology, Johnny Gibbons was ministering here at home. He has preached in a number of neighboring islands. His command of both French and English is nothing short of stunning, and he has earned the love, respect and admiration of our community. I venture that today, this shy, gentle, caring St. Martiner has a grasp, an understanding, of the scripture that is unsurpassed by most ordained Ministers in these Antilles, and yet the officials of his church, the Methodist Church, have not seen fit to invest him with ministerial authority.

Nothing was left out of his unscripted but deeply inspired eulogy—neither the remarkably enduring friendship of his uncle with Mayor Fleming nor gratitude, appreciative awareness, the thanks he extended to all of those who had assisted in the caring for his ill, disabled uncle over the years.

He left nothing unsaid in his amazing remembrance, nothing except the exemplary, loving devotion of a nephew who has spent the prime of his early manhood, twenty-odd years of his life, caring for an ill and disabled uncle.

Nothing else was left unsaid in his heart-wrenching eulogy except for the love, the gratitude and the proud admiration of this uncle for his nephew. Of that we are certain, for as we know our friend Trene, his Spirit was surely rejoicing all through the service, rejoicing to be Home, Home at last. Rejoicing and maybe thinking: "Surely goodness and mercy will follow my Johnny all the days of his life, for he dwells in the House of the Lord."

# The Silence is Deafening: In Praise of Dr. Hubert Petit

(*The Daily Herald*, July 11, 2006)

For Michel Petit and François Petit

The Doc has departed and the silence is deafening. Now we must look at photographs of him, like those printed in several newspapers since his passing, like the one on this page where he is seen greeting Dutch dignitaries: Lt. Governor Japa Beaujon is on his right; Mr. Félix Choisy, Mr. Jacques Deldevert and Mr. Walter G. Buncamper are on his left. These are five major personalities, each one of them worthy at the very least, of a solid chapter in any modern social history of this island. The Doc has departed. We can no longer speak *to* him. We can only speak *of* him.

During the last five years or so, on more than one occasion, he had asked me to come and chat with him, and every time I thought of going to meet with him on the Fort Hill, I would defer my visit, put it off with the same inept and insipid reasoning that went, more or less, as follows: The old man looks in shape, he is a doctor—one of the best—and he is surrounded by sons who are doctors and, like him, among the best. There is no rush, I have lots of time. I will speak with him later. Didn't my mother, whom he rescued from a sure mid-life death, live to be eighty-six? Surely the Doc will make it well beyond that. Then, on July 2, at about midday, I was informed that the Doc had left us.

The Greek writer-philosopher Aristocles, better known as Plato, informs us that his wise master, who loved to talk to everyone he met, placed no faith at all in writing, which is why he never wrote anything. He had no confidence at all in dead ink marks on parchment, no trust whatsoever in voiceless signs devoid of presence, in ink marks that cannot entertain our questions, that cannot answer, that cannot frown or smile and if need be reply: "No! That is not what I mean at all. You have misunderstood me. I must be doing a poor job explaining. Let me try to put it differently."

Obviously and fortunately for us readers, Plato did not follow his wise master that far in his idealism, but Socrates' point comes rushing home like a nauseating silent flight of bats every time someone leaves me forever and reality sets in—the realization that live exchange is no longer possible. Therein lay, I think, the outrageous, the scandalous limitation of these dead ink marks of mine, as opposed to the living, breathing presence of speech.

The Doc was an excellent physician, a superb surgeon. He was a pioneering medical practitioner on Saint-Martin and on neighboring islands. From 1959 to 1977, he was also the Mayor of St.- Martin. Those of us old enough to recall the acrimonious realities of politics in those days will agree that being mayor was as tough a job then as it must be today.

Like all human beings, the Doc had his weaknesses, his faults. Like most of us I'm sure there were some acts he must have regretted, some words he wished he could have retracted, but most St. Martiners will agree that he was a most exceptional human being, one of the brightest stars to have shined among us, if not *the* brightest.

E. M. Cioran notes that in our journey through life, there are those who applaud our snickering and giggling. They encourage us to bask in our smugness and in the apparent simplicity of our existence. They are wonderfully debilitating. Indeed! And there are others like the Doc, more demanding of us. They refuse to cater to our snorting. They force us to look further, to probe deeper, into the mysteries of life. They are painfully invigorating.

For this very private man who speaks to us in a deep and challenging poem dated significantly one year and one day after September 11, 2001, there is obviously no beginning, no end, no boundaries, no limits, but there are storms like those he overcame, the joy of giving and receiving, and most of all, there is endless hope, boundless optimism.

Like the stars that appear, journey a while, and then vanish in the void, he left us for what he calls "the bottomless pit of Eternity." Below is my translation, or rather my inadequate rendition, of his stunning French prose.

# Midnight, Zero Hour

Before midnight, when the loveliest stars imprint the sky, I gaze at Infinity and trust in Eternity.

I know not whence I came or where I am headed, but I know that I have traveled a bit of Infinity and shall depart for Eternity. The spark of my life will go out in the bottomless pit of eternity.

As fleeting as it will have been, I will have loved it very much. I look at it as a star-filled sky in which the stars are the bits of happiness I have received or that I have given. I can name some of them, but most are nameless.

Like the clouds that have never smothered the stars, the storms that have stricken my life have vanished without dimming my stars of joy.

At midnight, the last day of my life, it will be zero hour in the life of another. May it be as beautiful as mine ...

Saint-Martin, September 12, 2002.

Hubert PETIT

# French Text of Poem As Published in *Le Pélican*

Minuit, Zéro Heure

Quand avant minuit, s'impriment au firmament les plus belles des étoiles, je contemple l'Infini et je crois à l'Éternité.

Je ne sais d'où je viens, je ne sais où j'irai, mais je sais que j'ai parcouru un bout de l'Infini et que je partirai pour l'Éternité. L'étincelle de ma vie s'éteindra dans le gouffre sans fond de l'Éternité.

Quelque éphémère qu'elle aura été, je l'aurai beaucoup aimée. Je la regarde et la compare à un ciel étoilé, les étoiles sont les bonheurs que j'ai reçus ou que j'ai donnés, si je peux en nommer certains, le plus grand nombre n'ont pas de nom.

Comme les nuages qui n'ont jamais éteint les étoiles, les tempêtes qui ont pu traverser ma vie se sont évanouies sans pâlir mes étoiles de bonheur.

Lorsque sonnera minuit, le dernier jour de

ma vie, il sera zéro heure de la vie d'un autre.
Qu'elle soit aussi belle que la mienne …

Saint-Martin, le 12 septembre 2002
Hubert PETIT

*Le Pélican* (4juillet 2006)

# Barack Obama's Chickens

(*The Daily Herald*, August 13, 2007)

To the Memory of Edgar Mittelholzer of Guyana (1909-1965) who "soaked himself of petrol and set himself alight, like a Buddhist monk in Vietnam."

With reference to Eugene Robinson's syndicated article "Are whites really prepared to vote for Obama?" (*The Daily Herald*, July 31, 2007), specifically to Robinson's conclusive statement: "By now he [Mr. Obama] has mostly put the question of his racial identity to rest. As he knew all along, he's black," I beg to differ with Mr. Robinson's assessment of Mr. Obama's predicament.

As long as Mr. Obama remained a "long shot" candidate, one with little or no chance of succeeding in the race for the nomination, the crucial question of Mr. Obama's racial representation of himself remained inconsequential or, at best, secondary. Now that his candidacy is beginning to be taken seriously, Mr. Obama's racial representation of himself will most likely be scrutinized.

In his writings and speeches, Mr. Obama has consistently represented himself as a "black man," as an "African American." In his lexicon, the terms are synonymous. The problem with such racial representation is that Mr. Obama is half-black and half-white. He is the offspring of a white woman and a black man. The fact that in the past, racists in the U.S.A., South Africa and in other parts of the world (including the Caribbean) regarded people of mixed races as black does not make them black.

Endorsing, going along with the labelling of a person of mixed race as "black" perpetuates the ignorance of the racists, an ignorance that belies genetic reality. This racist labelling has the very pernicious effect of negating the non-black heritage of the mixed race person. In this case, it is as if Mr. Obama is trying to rub away the white component of his genetic makeup, as if he wishes to rub out his white mother, along with all her/his white relatives. Such an attitude usually denotes acute alienation, a profound failure to come to grips with one's identity.

Mr. Obama's representation of himself as "black" is therefore of crucial importance. Why doesn't he represent himself as a person of mixed race? Better, why doesn't he simply represent himself as a *person?* Those are fundamental questions that Mr. Obama will now have to address at the risk of alienating white, black and mixed-race voters. Barack Obama's *chickens are now coming home to roost.**

*This idiomatic expression which some St. Martiners were not acquainted with when my article appeared in *The Daily Herald* (in August 2007) became quite familiar to everyone after the infamous recorded outbursts of the Rev. Jeremiah Wright got released in March 2008. My usage of the expression, seven months before the *You Tubes* first surfaced, was just an uncanny coincidence.

For the reader of my *Ramblings*, it is more significant to note the following sequence of events: It was only following criticism and attacks in the press decrying certain things Mr. Obama said in his speech on race, specifically when he equated the reaction of his white grand mother with the recorded outbursts of the Rev. J. Wright, that Mr. Obama and his handlers began referring to the Senator's white relatives (to his grand mother, to his mother and to his grand father).

Today (late October, 2008,) revisiting my article and looking back at the campaigns, I wonder if, paradoxically, the success of Senator Obama's campaign was not considerably enhanced by his reactions to the Rev. Wright's outbursts, coupled with Senator McCain's decision to refrain from using the Rev. Wright's affair in his campaign against Senator Obama.

# This Old Sailor: Remembering Raymond "Tonton" Petit

*(The Daily Herald, November 1, 2007)*

For Ray Peterson and Roger Petit

It's all over now; the storm has finally lifted. The wind is a gentle breeze, the sea is oil poured forth. The sloop is nowhere to be seen; her old skipper has disappeared into the sunset.

For the last few years, he had lived apart from us, as if unbeknownst to him, his goddess of the dawn, his "Bella Aurora" had drifted away with him, away from our shoreline, into deeper, darker waters, into a world all of his own.

In this new world of his, the essence of his character still oozed forth; the sweetness of the boy that had budded and bloomed into the man, exuded. Still physically among us, it was as if faith had willed an end to all dialogue with us, for though he continued to smile and his eyes still sparkled, he could no longer entertain our questions.

A year or two before the drifting began, he was viciously attacked and gun wiped by an intruder as he tried to get out of his bed in a daring effort to put up some resistance. Ever since that unfortunate and most unspeakable aggression, it had been a downhill slide.

For the past three years or so, every time I thought of him adrift in that world of his, I would imagine my disarray, the sense of utter helplessness, all the pain that would ensue from visiting him and not being able to chat with him. I preferred remembering him as I had seen him the last time we had spoken.

We were seated on the terrace of "La Vie en Rose." He wore blue shorts and was sporting his skipper's cap. He complained that "they" had taken away the keys to his car and had ceased asking him to go fishing with them. I listened and offered no comment, for I knew that both his driving and his sea outings had become much too risky.

Mr. Raymond Petit, "Tonton Raymond" for some of us, was a gentle human being whose radiant smile and hardy laughter never failed to delight his friends and guests. He was a charming man who valued friendship, music and dialogue particularly.

Like with most of us, I'm sure there are some persons that Tonton disappointed, some acts he regretted, some words he wished he had not spoken, but those of us who knew the man and are old enough to recall the acrimonious realities of life in St. Martin, the fervour and excesses of the clans, will all concede that Mr. Raymond Petit was always way above the fray.

Like his father Mr. Jules Petit, Tonton was a seaman

at heart. I enjoyed listening to him speak of fishing and sailing, of the weather, of the banks and currents; of all things related to the sea. I especially relished listening to him reminisce about his adventures, the days when, as a young man, he sailed his "Bella Aurora." When he ventured away from sea talk, it was almost always to recollect dear, departed friends. All of that is now forever gone.

The last few years before he began to drift away from us, celebrating his birthday had become an event I looked forward to. Most of his friends and almost all of his family would be present. His wife Josette and his sister "Tante Éliane" would spoil us with their drinks and snacks as we listened and sang along to the strumming of the delightful duo, the "Cucaracha Kids," to the guitar music of Tonton and his fishing-music companion Mr. Jan Beaujon. "Guantánamera, Las mañanitas, La Cucaracha, and Adieu foulard, adieu madras" were among their favourite tunes as I recall.

A month or so ago, with some prodding from his wife, I mustered enough courage to visit Tonton at his home in Marigot. It was almost as I had imagined. He didn't recognize me at first, but when he heard my voice, a faint smile came upon his face and his eyes lit right up, as if they radiated all the light his broken body could gather to greet me.

After my visit, as I walked back to my jeep on the water front, Tonton's gaze was still on me and his strumming-singing filled my ears, as if it had never really ceased, as if to remind me that words, spoken or written, are not the only way to dialogue. Indeed! Light, music and love can also take us there.

In the cruel month of October 2007, just before the rains started marching down from Marigot Hill, death came to take Tonton Raymond away from all of us who loved him. But the old skipper was not home. His spirit had long since drifted away into the sunset.

# Autonomy and its relationship to English usage on this island

*(The Daily Herald,* November 15, 2007)

For Jacqueline Hamlet-Lubino

In *The Daily Herald* of November 10, 2007, we are informed that the *National Geographic* rates island [St. Martin] "in serious trouble." The Dutch side is "a mess." The French side "looks great by comparison." On page 14 of the inserted "St. Maarten Our Pride and Joy," Mr. Vance James echoes the point of view of those who wrote the article for the *National Geographic Traveler.* He decries Dutch St. Maarten while praising French St. Martin. He writes: "The French already have their new status. We the Dutch are not yet there." He concludes: "We have a problem and it is a leadership problem."

With all due respect to those "experts in sustainable tourism and destination stewardship," to Mr. Vance James and to all of those who keep praising French St. Martin while blaming or even denigrating Dutch St. Martin, I submit the following for their consideration: Empowerment—by that I mean the relative degree of autonomy that already exists on Dutch St. Martin—is far more vital to the survival of St. Martiners, both French and Dutch St. Martiners, and to the future of the entire island than all the ills and the mess outlined in the *National Geographic Traveler.*

As I assess the present situation, Dutch St. Martiners are one generation (20-25 years) ahead of us French St. Martiners in their common and most fundamental quest for autonomy or self-government. As for the road infrastructure (the only area in which French St. Martin may be said to be ahead of Dutch St. Martin), once funding becomes available it could be improved to surpass that of French St. Martin in a relatively short period of time, three or four years at most. Most of the roads on Dutch St. Martin are wider than those on French St. Martin, thereby allowing for overtaking and smoother traffic.

English, the language of St. Martiners, is the cement that binds islanders (both French and Dutch St. Martiners) into a people by enabling them to form, express and communicate thoughts and feelings. English is flourishing in Dutch St. Martin. In French St. Martin, English is a lame duck, a "canard boiteux," limping down a "cul-de-sac," literally the "ass of a bag" or a dead-end road. This wretched lame duck is limping toward the only shelter that remains on that desolate dead-end road: a Chinese restaurant. But faith has so willed it that as long as English flourishes on Dutch St. Martin, there will remain some hope for this entire island.

Autonomy, self-representation or self-government, is impossible outside of language. In St. Martin (French and Dutch St. Martin), autonomy is not feasible outside of English. But English on St. Martin has always been and continues to be a huge thorn in the posterior of successive European administrators, both French and Dutch. No wonder, then, that Dutch European officials, who, for some while, have been somewhat less adamant than their French counterparts, are now falling back into line with them in refusing to speak English to journalists. (See Mr. Marcel Gumbs' recent Letter to the editor in *The Daily Herald.*)

# The Masquerade Continues

(*The Daily Herald*, April 5, 2008)

For Allen Habib and Jean-Pierre Habib

There was something profoundly disturbing, fundamentally unfair, about a mixed-race candidate representing himself as "Black" while, at the same time, arguing that others should get beyond talking about race in an electoral campaign. That, however, was Senator Obama's position; part of his campaign strategy, before he felt obliged to deliver his speech on race.

Eight months ago, in my "Barack Obama's Chickens" (*The Daily Herald*, August 13, 2007,) I tried to address Senator Obama's misrepresentation of himself as "black" or "African American." I argued that as the son of a white woman and a black man, therefore genetically a person of mixed race—neither black nor white—Mr. Obama was either disingenuous or acutely alienated. I concluded that the "chickens would soon come home to roost."

The birds were finally routed recently when excerpts from jeremiads of the Rev. Jeremiah Wright, Mr. Obama's pastor and mentor for some twenty years, drove some of them home to their roost with a vengeance. In an effort to contain the negative fallout from the release of those excerpts, the Senator was forced to make a so-called "major speech on race."

In this speech, to his credit, Senator Obama called for an earnest discussion of race. Now, instead of continuing to refer to Mr. Obama as a "black" or "Afro-American candidate," some journalists can finally put forth *the* question without risking being accused of fomenting racial unrest or being labelled a racist. This question is simple but fundamental: "Mr. Obama, you are the offspring of a white woman and a black man. Why, then, do you represent yourself as black?" As long as Mr. Obama is not made to answer this question, our pseudo-black candidate, his handlers and syndicated columnists such as Eugene Robinson will continue to have a free ride.

A few years before his untimely passing in 1963, Dr Frantz Fanon, a Martiniquan of mixed race, a psychiatrist, the author of *Black Skin, White Masks* among other classics, explained that he had abandoned the ideology of "Négritude" for a "non-racist humanism." To some extent, Fanon's tormented life can be viewed as the product of a subtle and deadly form of racism: the labelling of a mixed race person as "black" and the psychic suffering, the agonizing struggle that ensued in societies (Colonial Martinique and France) polarized by race.

Obviously, not only do Senator Obama and his handlers endorse such racist labelling, they have succeeded in capitalizing on it. They have snared a black electorate that was squarely for the Clintons. This electorate is now wallowing in the fiction of this so-called "black candidacy" thereby setting the stage for a potential backlash from the white majority.

For the time being, all is swell and dandy in the fairyland of the Democrats. The elegant, ivy-league, clear-skin "black" candidate is the ideal psychic ointment for a guilt-ridden white electorate. But given the racial makeup of the U.S. electorate and its latent polarization along racial (black-white) lines, how long can this masquerade continue? *

*As of today, October 26, 2008, a few days before election day, and five days before my sixty-fourth birthday (just in case anyone might care) it appears almost certain that Senator Obama will defeat Senator John McCain to become the next president of the US. The polarization along racial (black-white) lines has not occurred thanks (I believe) to an electorate that seems more concerned with the still ongoing economic meltdown than with race baiting, so much the better. All is well that ends well.

But I suspect that the question of Mr. Obama's misrepresentation of himself will not go away. To the contrary, if or rather, when he is President, it will most likely become more pressing, more insistent. When that happens, let us hope the American media that is poorly informed in such maters will turn to Caribbean history, culture and literature, to Caribbean literature of English and French expression in particular, for more informed answers to these important questions. The media may then begin where Frantz Fanon left off.

As for my take on Senator Obama, I still believe that he is either disingenuous or acutely alienated. It is also possible that he is both. But I hasten to concede that there remains an enigma: How can a man with such kind eyes, such a sweet smile and such a soothing voice be either alienated or disingenuous?            •

Today, June 4, 2009, on line, I learned that two prominent French Caribbean writers, two of our best and brightest, Patrick Chamoiseau and Edouard Glissant have addressed a co-authored text, *L'intraitable beauté du monde* ... (The Uncompromising Beauty of the World) to Barack Obama back in January of this year. If you read French, please see (on line) Rosa Moussaoui's interview of Patrick Chamoiseau for *L'Humanité* ("Glissant-Chamoiseau: un regard aigu sur Barack Obama"). See particularly the commentary written by "Alain" posted on Wednesday, January 21, 2009: "J'exècre cette utilisation du mot "noir" concernant Obama ..." (I abhore this usage of the word "black" concerning Obama ...) And the writer lays forth, with an eloquence worthy of envy, why the word "black" to designate Obama is indicative of the enormous task that lies ahead in the U.S.A. Indeed, I truly do not understand how two such men (Glissant and Chamoiseau) whose lives and writings are so informed on this issue, so promising for the future of race relations in the Caribbean and in the world could refer to Mr. Obama as a "négro-africain".

# Like Sea Grape Wood: Remembering Mr. Élie G. Williams

(*The Daily Herald, February 10, 2009*)

To the Memory of Mr. and Mrs. Charles Williams

Looking at the photograph of my friend, the late Mr. Élie G. Williams in the published announcement of his passing, I could hardly contain my emotion. Strange the way an image, the eyes, the mighty sense of sight can overwhelm us, and in a second or so, trigger a flood of mental images, and of emotions buried among thousands of other events and occurrences spanning over half a century or more.

As a somewhat unruly boy growing up in Sandy Ground in the fifties, in the old Sandy Ground, I remember being reprimanded more than once by Mr. Charles Williams, Mr. Élie's father. And as soon as he would walk away from me, his wife, Mrs. "Mimi" Williams would find a way to smooth over the scolding of her husband. She always had something kind to say to me and she would always offer me something to eat and drink.

That's how it was in the Sandy Ground of my childhood. The men seemed distant and stern and the women were always there, strong, thoughtful and kind. Days were longer, people moved about slower and living was so much sweeter than today. Doors were left open. No one stole anything, but there was not much worth stealing in the Sandy Ground of my youth.

That is where Mr. Élie grew up into a lean, handsome young man, as tough as those pond-side-sticks he used for bracing the wire of his fish pots; as generous as sea grape wood, and the mangrove and Tamarind woods. Those were the most generous, the toughest woods; they released the most energy; they gave off the strongest, the best heat needed to prepare my mother's brick oven for the baking of the breads, and the puddings and tarts.

All of that was before Mr. Élie went abroad to try and better his lot in life and later returned home to settle down in his profession of house painter until his retirement some years ago.

There are some persons Mr. Élie may have disappointed, some others he might have wronged, but he was a man whose heart was so generous, that he could never have succeeded in pleasing everyone. And who among us is perfect? Which one of us is without sin?

Mr. Élie was a kind man. He was loyal to his family and friends as best he could. He was a decent, charming man, the essence of discretion and of generosity. Is that why the ladies loved him?

The Williams were our neighbours, but they were also relatives, family. My mother always reminded me that we were related to the Williams through her mother, my grandmother, Mrs. Aurélie Augustine Williams.

In the early fifties, I was eleven or twelve years old. One afternoon, I bit into the stem of one of the leaves of an enormous green plant that stood in front of a neighbour's house. I was so severely poisoned by the sap in that stem that

I almost died. Mr. Élie, then a young man in his early thirties, came home late that evening. I was told that when he saw me all swollen and near death, he "lost it": he went right out into the night onto the neighbour's property and uprooted the enormous plant.

Reminiscing those days, relating this incident now and here, talking about the old Sandy Ground, I cannot help feeling that I am forcing my "old stories" on hurried impatient readers, on people with all kinds of more pressing, more important concerns, on people with no time for this kind of talk. I feel that I am imposing. But all I truly wish to do here is to praise my old departed friend.

Indeed, why I'm I writing down these words if not out of a sense of profound gratitude for having known him, and of deeply felt loss; of utter despair -the loss of all hope- the sense that he is gone, forever gone, like the old Sandy Ground and all its old-timers, like all the old-timers of this land, like all old-timers everywhere since the beginning of time.

The poet sings: "I know that Creation is a big wheel that cannot turn without crushing someone, that birds must lose their feathers and flowers their sweet scent; that leaves must fall and that people must die, but let me cry."

Let me cry, indeed, I am not ashamed of crying. Let me weep, with all his loved ones, the departure, the passing, the death of my old friend and relative, the late Mr. Élie G. Williams.

# Four Letters to the Editor

In 1974, I moved to Québec, Canada and settled in the Montréal area where I found employment as a teacher and could pursue my education at McGill University. I share the concerns of French Canadians for their language and culture in Anglophone North America, but though bilingual, I've always felt somewhat of an outsider in Québec. But then again I don't recall reaching out to French Canadians the way I should have done. I regret not doing so. I still didn't hesitate, during the early eighties, to publicly voice my opinion on certain events. I have selected four pieces to the Montreal *Gazette* from that era to include in my rambling.

**'Withdrawal from the Sinai was moving experience'**
*The Gazette*, late April or early May 1982

To the memory of Paul Tutton and Elsa Sisto and for all my former colleagues at Western Laval High School in Chomedey, Laval

As I watched the numerous filmed reports of the long and difficult withdrawal from the Sinai, I was moved by something that I could not at first identify. But soon it became clear to me that what was moving me was something very beautiful and highly civilized about the way the people of Israel, soldiers and protestors went about their agonizing tasks.

Not once in all those filmed reports did I see a violent act perpetrated. Sure, there was a lot of pushing and shouting and even some kicking on the part of some protestors trying to break loose, but never any brutal violence committed by Jews against Jews.

There was no clubbing, shooting or knifing. Had there been any, I'm sure that the newsmen would have caught it and filled our screens with it.

No, this was not our North American-made violence, even though this is a country at war where fear is real and guns are everywhere.

There was something poignantly sad and healthy in that scene of the army officer weeping and consoling the protestor.

What struck me most in all those filmed reports was the efficiency with which the soldiers used dynamite on buildings, in contrast to the slow, awkward gentleness with which they subdued the protestors. I think Spinoza would have commended his people.

**'Media should lay off knocking Claude Ryan'**

*The Gazette*, June 25, 1982

For Mina Wittendal and Betty Le Maistre

I'm hopping mad. I've just finished reading Graham Fraser's

June 8 column on Claude Ryan's "tragic" predicament.

Why the obsessive political gossiping with regard to Mr. Ryan's leadership? Why the repeated attempts to discredit a decent man who has the courage to fight for his principles and refuses to sink to the lowest common denominator we have grown accustomed to in the North American political arena?

If Mr. Ryan is a tragic character, and I believe he is one, it is not because he is inflicted with a "special kind of blindness," as Mr. Fraser puts it. Tragic heroes are not blind. They are conscious. And it is precisely this awareness, this consciousness that is the essence of their tragic state.

To my knowledge, Mr. Ryan has not "scorned the problems of public opinion." He has argued that he will not let himself be packaged and sold like toothpaste or ketchup. A person is not a product, notwithstanding what the gurus of marketing might maintain.

So Mr. Ryan refuses to be packaged. Does that make him "vain"? And he didn't kneel and ask Bill Cusano to please vote with him on the motion of the *Parti Québécois* condemning the federal constitution plan. He preferred to let Mr. Cusano and others vote their conscience. Does that make him "proud"?

When Mr. Fraser cites an example such as the Cusano incident to illustrate his assertion that Mr. Ryan has a "curious streak of vanity," he lapses into what Mr. Ryan might refer to as "wallowing in trivia."

Mr. Fraser writes that Mr. Ryan "seems doomed to humiliation if he fights to stay on." "Humiliation" implies shame, disgrace, abasement. Mr. Ryan has done nothing to be ashamed of. It is those pusillanimous Liberal MNAs who should be ashamed of themselves for constantly mouthing off to journalists instead of attending to the people's business. I say Mr. Fraser and the press in general should stop defaming Claude Ryan.

**'New independence referendum should be demanded'**
*The Gazette*, April 4, 1983

For all my former colleagues at Chomedey Polyvalent High School, in Chomedey, Laval

Recently, Premier Lévesque announced in the National Assembly that the next provincial election will deal with the "national question." Liberals and "péquistes" applauded.

I think the Liberals had better cease applauding this idea of an election campaign in which the question of independence would be put to Quebecers. Rather, they should demand nothing less than a referendum with its appropriate referendum campaign and a clearly stated question on independence.

In the 1980 referendum, the ambiguity resulted from the way in which the question was put. This time around, it appears that the question may be clear enough: "Are you in favour of independence for Québec?"

That's how Doris Lussier suggests the question be put to the voters. Mr. Lussier is a high priest of independence, one of the architects of the 1980 referendum question. When he speaks, the "péquistes" strategists listen.

In an article in *La Presse*, Mr. Lussier states that it is imperative that this time around the question be clearly put. He states that he fully agrees with Vincent Prince, who argued in a *La Presse* editorial that a provincial election can in no way take the place of a referendum.

So what does Mr. Lussier suggest? "Let there be an electoral campaign on independence, but on the day of balloting, let there be two things: the election of a government and a referendum on independence. It will not cost any more money, everyone will be happy and no one will be able to contest the validity or the meaning of the result."

But while clearing up the question to be put, Mr Lussier has muddied up the campaign that would lead to the putting of the now clear-enough question. And why would he go to all this trouble? Maybe he knows that his strategy could cripple the Liberals by placing the federal Quebec Liberals, the Big Guns, at a great disadvantage.

In an electoral campaign on the question of independence as advocated by Mr. Lussier, federal Quebec Liberals could be painted as outsiders interfering in a provincial electoral campaign. Indeed, this is the image that the "péquistes" have been pushing all along.

In many ways, provincial Liberals are aiding and abetting the "péquistes" through their relative silence on this matter and their propensity to be openly critical of their federal colleagues.

Liberals working at the provincial level should not fall into the trap Mr. Lussier and his fellow strategists of the "Parti Québécois" are setting. They should not allow the péquistes to get away with the big lie, i.e., the painting of Quebec Liberals working at the federal level as "vendu(e) s" and outsiders.

This is no time for Liberal infighting. The stakes are too high. Liberals should demand that there be a referendum with its appropriate referendum campaign and a clear question (Mr. Lussier's question would do).

An electoral campaign on independence as advocated by Mr. Lussier will not do. Liberals should demand a referendum and they should set about crushing the big lie.

**'Lévesque's independence election ploy is foxy move'**

*The Gazette*, May 5, 1983

For Germain Thibodeau and Allen Enkin

Which is more irresponsible, the strategy Premier Lévesque has cooked up to try to remain in office while fulfilling his promise to have the next provincial election on independence, or the strategy Mr. Pierre Bourgault would have him adopt to declare independence? (Column, April 23)

Which is more irresponsible, "burying the hope of independence" like a squirrel buries nuts, or arguing that a majority of seats (even without a majority of the popular vote) is enough to declare independence, as Mr. Bourgault implicitly argues?

Mr. Bourgault writes: "I don't propose to discuss the merits of the system; I just state the plain fact." Why doesn't he discuss the merits of his system of declaring independence based on a majority of seats, as opposed to the merits of Mr. Lévesque's independence mandated by a majority of votes?

Could it be that there is no merit at all to Mr. Bourgault's system? Could it also be that he would have to explain the difference between a provincial election and a referendum on independence?

I believe Mr. Lévesque is more responsible than Mr. Bourgault. If the federal government agrees to abide by the results of this dangerous idea of a provincial election/referendum, which I doubt, and if it still takes place and Mr. Lévesque wins with 49 percent of the vote, he won't be trapped, as Mr. Bourgault puts it. He will have been elected without a mandate to declare independence.

Such a strategy is not irresponsible and stupid, as Mr. Bourgault would have us believe. It is foxy and squirrel-like. Squirrels do not bury nuts for keeps. They merely store them away until a later day.

# To Family and Friends

***

## November Poem for Martha Anne Reagan
## (In the Shadow of W. Stevens, 1986)

The leaves have fallen, Martha
They turned on their branches
And then they turned on themselves
On their way to the ground
By mid-Spring they'll have climbed back up
their limbs
Green -Red –Orange
They'll keep turning
And turning
Yellow-Brown
And then again
They'll start falling
Turning on themselves again
Nothing ever ends, Martha
Like leaves, we turn
And turn and turn
There must be a plan
We don't understand, Martha
Let's choose Love!
Love makes everything turn
And turn and turn
Like our poem, Martha.

# Lettre à Raymond Vialenc

11150, Chemin Meighen,
Pierrefonds, Québec, 29 décembre 1993

Mon cher Raymond,

Hier, 28 décembre - la triste nouvelle - du décès de ton père m'est parvenue. Un tel retard en pareille circonstance, c'est, sans doute, la rançon de l'absence, « the price I pay for living so faraway from Home. »

Mon cher Raymond, je n'ai pu être là pour vous présenter mes condoléances de vive voix (à Mme Vialenc, à toi, à Gérard, à Malou et autres membres de la famille) mais je tiens à ce que vous sachiez que ma pensée est avec vous.

Je le revois, ton père, cet homme chaleureux et bon, si prompt au sourire. J'entends son rire éclatant de vie. Puisque c'est ainsi, puisque même ici, sous ce ciel gris de décembre, je revois son sourire, puisque nous entendons son rire, toi et moi et Gérard et Malou et tant d'autres, c'est qu'il n'est pas tout à fait absent. N'est-ce pas, Raymond? N'est-ce pas?

Courage mon cher Raymond et très sincères condoléances. P.S. : Désormais c'est toi « le vieux »!!!

Your old pal,
Gérard

# Letter to the Daniels

Sainte-Anne-de-Bellevue, October 12, 1997.

Dearest Joseph, Jacqueline and Angèle:

These early days in October, the colors of the leaves are still turning. Soon, any time now, they'll start turning on themselves on their way to the ground. By late next spring they'll have climbed back up their branches, magnificent and green.

It seems that only yesterday we were all together near what was left of "Budds" after his spirit had left it. I meant to write to you much earlier, but I did not find, make, or take the time. I'm sorry, I'm sorry.

I'll always remember Budds the way I used to see him when I was a boy in Sandy-Ground (after I had met Joe and "whopped" his butt) and later during my visits back home. I'll remember him also as I saw him the last time I visited with him.

I was seated on the leather chair facing, across the living room area, the photograph of a handsome MP who, incidentally, is just as handsome and young today—provided he wears his cap. I was, of course, sipping on the punch.

As we reminisced about Élise's fried fish and Johnny-cakes, and Dion's jumbies, having noticed how tired and frail he had become, I remember thinking that I had better concentrate on the eyes and the voice and the smile of this old man I admired so much and so secretly during my fatherless youth.

All the reasons for such admiration echoed in the beautiful words spoken by Ted with such brevity, eloquence and clarity; honesty, integrity, love of and dedication to family, as I recall. Granddaughters reading from the Book were the perfect confirmation of the words spoken.

Dearest Angèle, Jacqueline and Joseph, these early days in October 1997, leaves are turning on themselves on their way to the ground. By next spring, they'll have climbed back up their limbs all glorious and green. Such is life, such is life; a never-ending turning, a troping that never ceases, not even in death.

Sincerely,
*Joua*

P.S. : Désormais, personne ne m'appellera plus *Joua*.

# Letter to Jeannine Marathon

Ste-Anne-de-Bellevue, April 5, 1998

Dearest Jeannine:

These early days in April up here in Québec, it's dark, damp and dreary, but soon the sun will return and drive away the darkness and the dampness and the sadness, and lilac shrubs, battered, bruised and broken by ice storms, will start budding. By late April or May, deep-green leaves and oval clusters of purple blooms will have hidden all the bruises.

By the first snowfall in December, having shed first their flowers then their leaves, the lilac shrubs will stand naked once again waiting for the frost. So it has been since the beginning of time; a never-ending cycle, a turning that never seems to end but in death.

Ever since (some months ago) I stopped by your office after Johnny's passing, I've been meaning to write you a few lines or to visit with you for a while and talk *about* my friend Johnny given that we can no longer talk *to* him. But I didn't make time to write or to visit. I'm sorry, I'm sorry.

My friend Johnny, your brother whom you knew so much better than I, was a sensitive, kind, intelligent, decent man. Like his friend Raymond, my brother who died a young man, I think Johnny grew up at a time when life in St. Martin was hard but so much more in tune with what some of us consider "the essentials," so much more humane than it became.

He went away an adolescent, and I believe that like most of us St. Martiners who lived abroad, he was torn apart by the uprooting, by the persistent call of the sun, the sea, the sand, and the splendour of his childhood.

When he returned home a gentle sophisticated man, I think he sought to recapture the warmth of earlier times and I know that he managed to recover some, thanks to you, but I feel that somehow life in St. Martin did not live up to his expectations.

During the year I spent in St. Martin after the death of my brother, I got to know Johnny fairly well, I think. A few months earlier, during a brief visit home, I had brought him the news of Raymond's death. He was visibly shaken and I remember being quite taken aback at the moment, for I had not expected his reaction; I didn't know that they had been old pals. This drew me closer to him.

I'm sorry I was not able to pay my respects the way I would have preferred, the way we used to once upon a time, but for whatever it is worth, I shall always associate my friend Johnny with his old pal (my brother Raymond); with gentleness; with kindness; with the loving relationship he had with you; with the loving, caring patience you had with him.

Dearest Jeannine, for whatever it is worth, I feel that we must not be sad when we think of Johnny, for his spirit now rests in peace where it dwells forever with those of his loved ones as in the splendour of childhood—there now forever. This I believe. This I feel we must believe.

# Cousin, quimbé raid!

Marigot le 15 janvier 2002

Cousin,

Ce soir, de ma table de travail, je vois les vieux murs du Fort Saint-Louis resplendissants dans la lumière et, tout près, de l'autre côté de la rue, le balcon de la triste vieille maison blanche de notre grand-père.

Je pense à toi dans ta détresse et te souhaite patience et force afin que tu puisses grimper ton morne douloureux jusqu'aux belles lumières du sommet.

J'ai pleine confiance en toi, toi qui as dû grimper tant de mornes raides depuis ce jour lointain et malheureux du décès de ta mère.

Je ne sais te dire combien cela m'a peiné de te voir la dernière fois que je t'ai vu à Grand-Case. Toi si loin, si inaccessible, moi si démuni, si brisé et ton vieil ami John accroché à la clôture, pleurant, pleurant comme on voyait pleurer ton petit Mao quand son père s'en allait.

Bientôt, quand tu reviendras, nous reprendrons nos vieilles drôleries … Tu me feras rire comme avant ton malheur.   Toute cette affaire ne sera qu'un méchant cauchemar : poussière dans le vent du temps, le temps qui règle tout.

La construction de ton mur est terminée. Il est solide comme tu l'as voulu, comme toi, comme il faut que tu sois.

Cousin!
Quimbé!
Quimbé raid!

# For Robert Romney

**April 2002:** (Still in the Shadow of W. Stevens)

**Remembering Mother's Day**

These last days in April, cedars in The
Savannah are shedding all their flowers ...
offerings to the wind.

Pink pearls are falling, turning in the wind,
turning on themselves on their way to the
ground.

Early next April, they'll be back up on their
branches, ravishingly pink.

Such is life, Robert—a troping that never
ceases.

Soon it will be Mother's Day, and I'll be
thinking of you on your first motherless
Mother's Day.

The cedar flowers are falling. If I could catch
them on their way to the ground, we could
fill up all the rooms in the old house in Sandy
Ground, if only she could see them, and smell
them and smile at us the way she used to.

Cedar flowers are falling, twisting in the wind, turning on themselves on their way to the ground.

Early next April, they'll be back up on their branches ravishingly pink.

Such is life Robert, a never-ending turning.

I'd like to be remembered - remembering Mother's Day- and these cedar flowers that are falling.

## August 16, 1990: *Spirit of the plains**

« *Et maintenant j'ai trop de peine*
*Les sept épées hors du fourreau*
*Sept épées de mélancolie … »*

Almost five
Sunlight is on the frame of *Spirit of the plains*
Soon it will bathe my naked lady
And I'll go with her through wet land
Amid wild flowers
Beneath the tall trees on the left
Through the thin green line
And the frame
And the window
Down to *the River of the Prairies*
Naked Lady of the Plains
On this sixteenth day of August
I'll be your sixteenth tall bird
We'll follow you down to the river
To watch the going down of the sun

*A print by Sidney Long

# The Toil of Beavers

For Nick Girolamo

At Pointe-des-Cascades, Vaudreuil-Soulanges, where I used to walk along the canal, and the trails, on down to the Point and the dam, I often wondered what beavers think (in as much as they do think) at night when their tree begins to groan and crack under their teeth, just before it comes crashing down on the bank.

My friend Nick is a gardener. I broached the subject to him once. Without the slightest hesitation, he quipped: "I don't think beavers think, but if you get close enough to them, listen well and you'll hear them shout: "Let's get the heck out of here!"

# Le labeur des castors

Pour Martine et Jacques Delsemme

À Pointe-des-Cascades, Vaudreuil-Soulanges, où je me promenais le long du canal et de la berge, jusqu'à la Pointe et le barrage, je me suis souvent demandé à quoi pensent les castors (en autant qu'ils pensent) la nuit lorsque leur arbre se met à geindre, à craquer sous leurs dents, avant de s'écrouler sur la berge.

Mon ami Nick, jardinier de métier, auprès de qui je m'étais renseigné m'a dit sans hésiter : « Je ne pense pas qu'ils pensent, les castors. Mais si vous les approchez, vous les entendrez s'écrier: Vite! Vite! Fichons-le-camps d'ici! ».

# Rambling on a Perfect Rambler: Alexis Leger-Saint-John Perse

To the Memory of Anne de Sales Aurandt Reagan (1943-1986)

"The man who thinks his homeland sweet is but a tender beginner; he to whom every country is like his own is already strong; but he only is perfect to whom the whole world is a foreign land."

—Hugh of Saint Victor*

*As quoted in (Todorov, 1982:311). Trans. (from the French): G. M. Hunt

In the biography he first published in 1972, the Guadeloupian - born French diplomat Alexis Leger, also known as the poet Saint-John Perse, and 1960 Nobel Laureate in literature mentions his ancestor, Charles-Gervais d'Ormoy or Dormoy who "joined the Conventional Government in order to help defend the islands against the British." (Saint-John Perse, 1972: X)

Though Leger only refers to this ancestor as a landowner in Saint-Barthélémy and in Guadeloupe, this "Conventionnel" is none other than Charles Dormoy, who was Commander of Saint Martin from 1798 to 1808.

Charles Dormoy is, indeed, the father of Pierre Georges Dormoy, the first Mayor of Saint-Martin. According to the inscription (written in English!) on his tomb in La Lotterie: "Peter Charles Dormoy, Born at Joiyny in the department of Yonne, departed life on the 12th of May 1818, aged 71 years."

In J.E. Richardson's *Story of Saint Martin*, we learn that it was Mr. Emmanuel Rey and Mayor Georges Dormoy who took the steps that made it possible for the children of the black population of St. Martin to begin to receive an education. I do not wish to negate or in any way minimize the good will and deeds of these gentlemen and their Council, but it is a fact that on February 4, 1794, the National Convention (September, 1792, to October 26, 1795) abolished slavery in all of the colonies. (Sévillia, 254: 2003) It most likely took a few years for this decree to become fully effective in Saint Martin.

Mr. Richardson also writes: "From the year 1838 to 1865, Saint Martin had for Mayor, a man whose name needs to be mentioned. He is no other than Mr Georges Dormoy, son of Charles Dormoy." The author then tells how Mayor Dormoy saved his country (Saint Martin) from a terrible scourge, namely the cholera that ravaged Guadeloupe and might have done the same to Saint Martin had Mayor Dormoy not quarantined a group of persons (including Commander Martin, his superior).

This group was returning to St. Martin from Guadeloupe. Mr. Richardson describes Mayor Georges Dormoy as a man who held that "[to] rule properly, gentleness is better than violence." Richardson adds that "he [Mr. Dormoy] was descended from a very honourable family, distinguished for their services rendered during the revolution." (Richardson: 1986).

Marie-René Alexis Leger, the son of Amédée Leger and Françoise-Renée Dormoy, was born in Guadeloupe in 1887. It was at home and later at the "Lycée of Pointe-à-Pitre" that the young Leger began his schooling and it was only in 1899, when Leger was twelve years old, that the family left Guadeloupe to settle permanently in Pau, France.

Even though he never returned to the French Antilles, where many of his relatives still resided, and though some accused him of disowning his past and his people, no matter where he found himself, Alexis-Leger-Saint-John Perse never ceased one way or another to refer to the West Indies where he was born and spent his childhood. His very rich and informative correspondence—and almost all of his poems—explicitly testify to the importance of his French-Caribbean origins and to a happy special childhood spent in Guadeloupe.

For Saint-John Perse as I read him, there is no line to be drawn between continents. Though very much in tune with his roots, both in Europe and in the Caribbean, he considered himself a sort of "nowhere man." This made him a kind of "everywhere man," someone who claimed to inhabit his name (Saint-John Perse), a name he gave himself. In doing so, he chose words, "nomadism," "traveling", "rambling" over settling-in.

# Une lettre inédite de Saint-John Perse à William Astor Chanler, Jr.

Pour Jade Hervé Marraud Vatblé de Sigalony

In his fairly recent "Méditations à Saint-John Perse," commenting poetically on a past critical, but so-called "necessary" reception of Saint-John Perse's poetry in the French Caribbean, Patrick Chamoiseau explains:

> (…) Nous n'avions pas besoin de vous [de Saint-John Perse] en ce temps-là … Nous vous opposions à Césaire … Césaire était l'esclave en lutte. Et vous étiez le Maître … Nous avions besoin de ces lectures très pauvres qui servaient de combustible aux luttes que nous menions. Nous ne savions pas à quel point cette lecture appauvrissait Césaire tout autant qu'elle vous appauvrissait … (Chamoiseau: 2006)

> (...) We did not need you [Saint-John Perse] in those days ... We used to place you in opposition to Césaire ... Césaire was the rebellious slave and you were the Master ...We needed those very poor readings that served as fuel for the battles we were waging. We didn't know how much this reading

was diminishing Césaire as much as it was diminishing you (...) (Translation: G.M.H.)

Indeed, during the nineteen sixties, seventies and eighties, for the overwhelming majority of French West Indian intellectuals, it was politically convenient to read Saint John Perse's poetry in opposition to Aimé Césaire's.

C'est un heureux hasard qui m'a permis de faire la connaissance de M. William Astor Chanler, Jr. (1904-2002), d'établir une très brève correspondance avec lui, et plus tard, de le rencontrer, chez lui, à Camden, dans le Maine.

Dans son petit livre, *And Did Those Feet in Ancient Time: A Seven Hundred Acre Island Reminiscence*, (Outerbridge Books, Rockport, Maine, 1984, 64p.) M. Chanler, Jr. nous conte la riche histoire de cette petite île du Maine, jadis

terre ancestrale de la Nation Penobscot, aujourd'hui et depuis plus d'un siècle, propriété privée de quelques riches familles américaines.

"For more than a decade, from 1942-55, Alexis Leger spent one or two months each summer on 700 Acre Island as mother's or my guest." («Durant plus d'une décennie, de 1942-55, Alexis Leger a séjourné un ou deux mois chaque été à Seven Hundred Acre Island en tant qu'invité de ma mère ou de moi-même »), écrit l'auteur. (p. 57)

En effet, dans une lettre prophétique à Mme Biddle, une amie américaine (épouse de Francis Biddle, « Attorney General » des États-Unis), lettre datée le 20 septembre 1942, Leger écrivait : « Je devrai beaucoup à cette île, où j'ai consommé déjà tant de solitude, et marché, de jour en jour, dans des songes plus riches que je ne jugerais bon aujourd'hui de m'en permettre » (*Œuvres complètes*, 1972: p.903). Une note à cette lettre nous apprend que c'est Mme Beatrice Astor Chanler, une autre amie américaine, qui lui avait ménagé, chaque année, l'accueil d'une propriété qu'elle possédait dans le « Penobscot Bay », sur les côtes du Maine.

C'est dans cette île que Leger séjourna plusieurs mois en compagnie de son amie la comtesse Marthe de Fels. (Lettre de W. A. Chanler, Jr. à G. Hunt) C'est sur Seven Hundred Acre Island, dans la maison des Chanler, qu'il acheva son poème *Vents* qui lui a valu, en 1949, un article élogieux de Paul Claudel dans la *Revue de Paris*. Dans son article, Claudel souligne l'importance des « horizons partagés » de SJP. Selon Claudel, les origines d'Alexis Leger; sa naissance « au beau milieu de la corbeille antillaise » font de lui un « homme de désir » (*Revue de Paris*, nov.1949 : p.6). Comme pour illustrer, confirmer ou souligner la perspicacité de Claudel, Saint-John, dans Amers (Strophe III), cisèlera le bel énoncé métaphorique aujourd'hui célèbre : « Le faucon du désir tire sur ses liens de cuir. »

Suivent une photographie de « Yellow Sands » : La maison d'été des Chanler, la photocopie (Pages 1 - 5) de la lettre manuscrite du « 16 Sept. 1944 » d'Alexis Leger à M. William A. Chanler Jr. et la transcription de la lettre dans son intégralité.

« Yellow Sands » : maison d'été des Chanler

Foo Deer Island, 16 Sept. 1944

Mon cher Willy

Je ne veux pas quitter votre Île
sans vous dire tout ce que je lui emprunte
de force et de santé pour mes épreuves à
venir, publiques ou privées — Tout ce
que je lui emprunte aussi de sérénité.

Je vous garderai toujours, à vous
et à votre Mère, une infinie gratitude
pour cette bénédiction du sort qu'aura
été pour moi, dans mon exil, ce triple
séjour en lieu si pur, à l'ombre de si
claires affections. Je suis particulièrement
heureux, cette année, de ne vous avoir
pas manqué à votre court passage sur l'Île.

J'étais encore fatigué, à mon
arrivée, et n'ai pu partager autant que
je me le proposais la vie physique de grand
air avec vous. Peu après votre départ

L'air vivifiant du Penobscot Bay avait ⟨2⟩
déjà opéré son miracle sur moi, et j'ai
repris à travers brouille mes courses, où ma
pensée vous rejoignait affectueusement sur
toutes les pistes que nous avions ensemble
recherchées, il y a deux étés.

Le côtre s'est admirablement comporté.
Sa coque est parfaitement saine et son gréement
seul aura besoin d'être révisé. J'en ai usé
parfois seul, et d'autres fois ~~avec les~~ ᴛᵒⁿⁱᵗᵃ, ᵖᵘⁱˢ ᵃᵛᵉᶜ
Bohn, qui aimaient beaucoup les sorties
en mer. Je n'ai jamais eu d'autres incident
que des écoutes rompues à renouer. Le bateau,
désarmé et halé, est maintenant à son
poste d'hivernage, tous les agrès et les épars
rentrés, ainsi que le canoë. Mais la bâche
de ~~cou~~ protection de la coque a été déchirée
par la tempête d'hier, et votre mère a dû
donner des instructions pour qu'elle soit réparée
ou remplacée.

Marion et Ted sont rentrés il y a
quelques jours. Ils ne sont pas sortis en
mer avec moi, Ted n'aimant pas ce sport,

3

et Marion ayant gardé le goût du round-boat.

J'ai fait l'inspection de vos clôtures
pour dégager Toutes celles Que menaçait la
végétation. Beaucoup de Supports sont rompus
par l'usure de la rouille au ras du sol. Votre
neveu voulait les faire remplacer. Je lui ai
dit qu'il valait mieux attendre la belle saison,
puisque ces clôtures pour l'instant ne servent
encore à rien.

L'appontement face à l'Est est
en très bon état, mais, pour le sauvegarder,
il faudra, à première occasion, remplacer
un support, vers le haut de l'escalier,
qui ne donne plus d'appui par suite d'éboulement
du sol à sa base.

J'ai inspecté à fond la ligne Téléphonique,
qu'il a fallu dégager et préserver en plusieurs
points. J'ai coupé, sur le parcours, quelques
branches hautes de sapins, consolidé ou redressé
quelques poteaux, et, vers la fin du parcours,
aux angles Nord-Ouest et Nord-Est, tout
près de la côte Nord, derrière la maison des
Norton junior, j'ai coupé à la scie (pour

4

éviter les chocs de la hache ) Trois sapins
abattus par le vent ~~qui~~ dont le fil téléphonique
supportait par miracle tout le poids. Il faudra,
au printemps, revoir tout cela, car quelques
poteaux ont perdu beaucoup de leur solidité,
et la ligne elle-même, en ces parages, demeure
très distendue.

Mon cher Willie, vous n'imaginez
pas quel arrachement est pour moi ce
départ de votre Île. Les derniers jours
de solitude affectueusement partagés avec
votre Mère, en un tel lieu, ont approfondi
encore en moi le sentiment de tout ce qu'on
y recueille d'exceptionnel, pour l'esprit,
le corps et l'âme. Ma pensée y retournera
souvent, à travers ~~tout~~ toutes vicissitudes
de ma vie à venir. Elle vous y retrouvera
toujours aussi proche, dans ma profonde
affection. Et moi-même j'espère pouvoir
vous y revisiter un jour librement, avant
ou après la joie de votre accueil en France.

(5)

Je vous embrasse, mon cher Willy, en vous adressant tous mes vœux attentifs et les plus affectueux, dignes de votre cœur d'homme et de votre belle nature virile, si généreuse en tout.

Je voyage avec votre mère jusqu'à New York et suis heureux de penser au visage éclairé de santé qu'elle vous rapporte. J'espère vous revoir avant trop longtemps, à New York ou à Washington. Bonne chance pour votre libération prochaine et la réorientation de votre vie civile !

De tout cœur

Alexis L.

*700 Acre Island, 16 Sept. 1944*

*Mon Cher Willy*

*Je ne veux pas quitter votre Ile sans vous dire tout ce que je lui emprunte de force et de santé pour mes épreuves à venir, publiques ou privées – Tout ce que je lui emprunte aussi de sérénité.*

*Je vous garderai toujours, à vous et à votre Mère, une infinie gratitude pour cette bénédiction du sort qu'aura été pour moi, dans mon exil, ce triple séjour en lieu si pur, à l'ombre de si claires affections. Je suis particulièrement heureux, cette année, de ne vous avoir pas manqué à votre court passage sur l'Ile.*

*J'étais encore fatigué, à mon arrivée, et n'ai pu partager autant que je me le proposais la vie physique de grand air avec vous. Peu après votre départ l'air vivifiant du Penobscot Bay avait déjà opéré son miracle sur moi, et j'ai repris à travers brousse mes courses, où ma pensée vous rejoignait affectueusement sur toutes les pistes que nous avions ensemble recherchées, il y a deux étés.*

*Le côtre (sic) s'est admirablement comporté. Sa coque est parfaitement saine et son gréement seul aura besoin d'être révisé. J'en ai usé parfois seul, et d'autres fois avec Tonita, puis avec les Bohn, qui aimaient beaucoup les sorties en mer. Je n'ai jamais eu d'autre incident que des écoutes rompues à renouer. Le bateau, désarmé et halé, est à son poste d'hivernage, tous les agrès et les espars rentrés, ainsi que le canoë. Mais la bâche de protection de la coque a été déchirée par la tempête d'hier, et votre Mère a dû donner des instructions pour qu'elle soit réparée ou remplacée.*

*Marion et Ted sont rentrés il y a quelques jours. Ils ne sont pas sortis en mer avec moi, Ted n'aimant pas ce sport, et Marion ayant gardé le goût du row-boat.*

*J'ai fait l'inspection de vos clôtures pour dégager toutes celles que menaçait la végétation. Beaucoup de supports sont rompus par l'usure de la rouille au raz (sic) du sol. Votre Mère voulait les faire remplacer. Je lui ai dit qu'il valait mieux attendre la belle saison, puisque ces clôtures pour l'instant ne servent encore à rien.*

*L'appartement face à l'Est est en très bon état, mais, pour le sauvegarder, il faudra, à première occasion, remplacer un support, vers le haut de l'escalier, qui ne donne plus d'appui par suite d'éboulement du sol à la base.*

*J'ai inspecté à fond la ligne téléphonique qu'il a fallu dégager et préserver en plusieurs points. J'ai coupé, sur le parcours, quelques branches hautes de sapins, consolidé ou redressé quelques poteaux, et, vers la fin du parcours, aux angles Nord-Ouest et Nord-Est, près de la côte Nord, derrière la maison des Norton junior, j'ai coupé à la scie (pour éviter les chocs de la hache) trois sapins abattus par le vent et dont le fil téléphonique supportait par miracle tout le poids. Il faudra, au printemps, revoir tout cela, car quelques poteaux ont perdu beaucoup de leur solidité, et la ligne elle-même, en ces parages, demeure très distendue.*

*Mon cher Willy, vous n'imaginez pas quel arrachement est pour moi ce départ de votre Ile. Les derniers jours de solitude affectueusement partagés avec votre Mère, en un tel lieu, ont approfondi encore en moi le sentiment de tout ce qu'on y recueille d'exceptionnel, pour l'esprit, le corps et l'âme. Ma pensée y retournera souvent, à travers toutes vicissitudes de ma vie à venir. Elle vous y retrouvera toujours aussi proche, dans ma profonde affection. Et moi-même j'espère pouvoir vous y revisiter un jour librement, avant ou après la joie de votre accueil en France.*

*Je vous embrasse, mon cher Willy, en vous adressant tous mes vœux attentifs et les plus affectueux, dignes de votre cœur d'homme et de votre belle nature virile, si généreuse en tout.*

*Je voyage avec votre Mère jusqu'à New York et suis heureux de penser au visage éclairé de santé qu'elle vous rapporte. J'espère vous revoir avant trop longtemps, à New York ou à Washington. Bonne chance pour votre libération prochaine et la réorientation de votre vie civile!*

*De tout cœur*
*Alexis L.*

# A Letter from Mr. William A. Chanler Jr. to Gérard M. Hunt

Penobscot Ave
Camden, Me,
0 4 8 4 5.

Mons. Gérard M. Hunt,        12 Aug. '85,
19, Place Andelot
Ville Lorraine, PQ
J 6 Z - 3 N 9

Dear Gérard;

Enclosed is a WW II - NY Times
item from Vichy, France re: "Vichy
declares Ex-official [Legal] left France
Legally." The year might be 1945.
I thought you might like this!

Also a thought on our late friend;
Countess Marie de Chabanne la Palice.
She often referred to her property in Tunis, NA,
when she was with us. But it was Leger
who really felt responsible, somewhat, for the
death of her son in Pekin, China, who had
been shipped out to replace Leger on the battle
transfer + holiday in the South Seas.
Leger sold his steeplechasing Mongolian

[2]

pony, a lively animal apparently,
to young Chabanne, who not long
after was killed riding Leger's pony
over a difficult jump on the race course
Leger in his younger days was originally
a good horseman & athlete.
    Glad to be of help.
      Sincerely,
      William Chaulo

# Questions portant sur la lettre du 16 septembre 1944 suivies des réponses de Monsieur William Astor Chanler, Jr.

**Question 1**: - ... *pour mes épreuves à venir, publiques ou privées* ... (lines 3-4)* Ordeals or tasks? Did he anticipate public or private ordeals you know of? *The line numbering applies to the manuscript, not to its transcription. Mon numérotage des lignes s'applique au manuscrit et non à sa transcription.

**Answer**: -He had employment as a French consultant at the Library of Congress. Meeting with various Prime Ministers of France, explaining the downfall of France, perhaps could be embarrassing.

**Q. 2**: -... *ce triple séjour* ... (lines 9-10) His third visit at 700 Acre Island?

**A.:** -Having visited Acre Island in 1942 and 1943, up to a month each summer avoiding the excessive heat of Washington, D.C. where he lived in Georgetown.

**Q. 3** : ...*votre court passage sur l'Ile* ... (line 13) What was the occasion? Can you recall the visit?

**A.:** -Yes! I obtained ten days' leave from the C. G. [Coast

Guard] where I was stationed and operating out of the Buoy Yard, Portsmouth, Va., O in C [Officer in Charge] of Buoy Tenders.

Q.4: - ... *toutes les pistes que nous avions ensemble recherchées, il y a deux étés*. (lines: 22-23) Quelles pistes? Please explain.

A.: - All the trails we found together two summers in a row, walking on 700 Acre Island.

Q. 5: - ... *Le côtre* (sic) ... (line 24) Your cutter? How big? Was he as good a sailor as one might infer from his letter? Please elaborate.

A.: - He enjoyed rowing and paddling an Adirondack guide Boat. Although he had chartered a trading schooner in Tahiti and knew how to sail, he preferred being a passenger rather than a navigator.

Q. 6: - ... *Tonita, les Bohn* ... (lines 27-28) Can you supply full names and/or any additional information?

A.: - Miss Tonita Orena, the descendant of the last Spanish colonial governor of California, visited me for a week or ten days during the summer of 1944 when I was home on leave, when she happened to be East. Mr. and Mrs. Bohn had the old Chapman cottage on 700 Acre Island.

Q. 7: - ... Marion et Ted ... (line 38) Same question as above.

A.: - Marion Dorn (designed fabrics) married to Ted

McKnight Kauffer, artist, who painted and designed War Posters during W.W. II for the army or U.S. government.

**Q.8**: - ...*Norton junior*, (line 63) same question as above.

**A.**: - Al, son of Sidney B. Norton, owner and operator of the yacht yard on 700 Acre Island ...

**Q. 9**: - *Les derniers jours de solitude affectueusement partagés avec votre mère*, ... This, I believe, speaks to Leger's deep appreciation of your mother's friendship and kindness. Could you elaborate on any impressions of or feelings about Leger your mother may have expressed to you?

**A.**: - Beatrice Chanler was an ardent Francophile. She was both a good listener and fluent in French herself, and a mutual friend of Marthe, Comtesse de Fels. Both were friends of Mildred and Ambassador Bliss of Washington. Beatrice had the greatest respect for and admiration of Leger's verses in the French original. She and the Biddles were only too glad to offer Leger relief from Washington D.C. heat. And what joy she had conversing with the great poet, on many subjects!

**Q. 10**: - ... *toutes vicissitudes de ma vie à venir* ... As in item and related question 1 above, one gets the impression that he anticipates problems in his *vie à venir*. Am I misreading? Can you add to your answer to question number 1?

**A.**: - At first, during the war, he had a limited visa given to him by F.D. Roosevelt—if he left U.S. boundaries, he could not gain re-entry. Only later (after De Gaulle withdrew temporarily from government) could he return to France.

**Q.11**: - *Je voyage avec votre Mère jusqu'à New York* ... Was there any special significance to this trip? Did he travel with your mother on other occasions? Please elaborate.

**A.**: - Beatrice Chanler was in fragile health and with a bad heart—it was an ordeal for her to get off the island with baggage and to catch the train in Rockland, changing trains in Portland. On this or on a second trip, Beatrice suffered a heart attack and Leger arranged to have her entered in a Boston hospital. He contacted the USCG [United States Coast Guard]. I was relieved of duty for ten days and given emergency leave to visit her.

Mme. Chanler dans son salon / Mrs. Chanler in her living room

# Voilà plus de vingt ans ...

Pour Caroline et Emilie Schoofs

Voilà plus de vingt ans que j'ai dû renoncer à un travail que j'envisageais entreprendre sur Alexis Leger/Saint-John Perse. Mon projet avait été approuvé par les autorités compétentes à l'Université de Montréal mais les aléas de la vie ne m'ont pas permis de poursuivre ma recherche.

Il y a donc presque vingt-cinq ans que je ne fréquente plus, de près, ni l'œuvre de Saint-John Perse, ni sa critique. D'autres ont sans doute apporté des réponses aux questions que je me posais à l'époque. La publication de ce vieux *Projet de recherche* ne se veut rien d'autre qu'un modeste témoignage de l'intérêt que j'ai porté jadis à l'œuvre incommensurable d'Alexis Leger/Saint-John Perse.

**Projet de recherche (Ph.D.) soumis au départment d'Études françaises de l'Université de Montréal en mai 1985**

1. TITRE : *Politique et poétique* : *l'antillanité de Saint-John Perse*
2. PROBLÈME : (hypothèse de travail; importance théorique et pratique de la recherche; objectif(s) de l'étude ...)

Dans une vaste « littérature » consacrée à Alexis Leger,

alias Saint-John Perse, il y a un manque. A quelques exceptions près, les Antilles ne sont mentionnées que comme étant le lieu exotique de la naissance du poète-diplomate. Il n'existe pas, à ma connaissance, d'étude systématique et approfondie visant à mettre en valeur une relation entre l'antillanité de Saint-John Perse, sa politique et sa poétique.

Comment peut-on être Créole antillais, homme politique français de premier plan et « grand » poète –tout cela à la fois- en Occident au XXe siècle? C'est là une question importante que l'œuvre de Saint-John Perse et sa réception semblent poser. J'émets l'hypothèse que l'antillanité de SJP s'inscrit dans une relation dynamique et dialectique avec sa politique et sa poétique, que son antillanité peut se définir en fonction de sa politique et de sa poétique. Leger, lui-même, a essayé de nier le rapport difficile entre poétique et politique, soit en voulant gommer toute différence entre les Antilles françaises et la France, soit en tirant un trait rouge entre le poète et le diplomate, entre Alexis Leger et le supposé Saint-John Perse. Dans ce travail, je tenterai de souligner ce qu'il a cherché à gommer et à rapprocher ce qu'il s'est efforcé de dissocier.

3. MÉTHODE (rapport avec les recherches déjà faites et la documentation existante; sources théoriques et originalité de la démarche; prévisions : plan, calendrier ...)

4. Ma lecture se voudra sociocritique, mais mon approche s'insèrera dans l'herméneutique de Gadamer; cercle critique symbole du dynamisme, de la dialectique,

du paradigme et de l'aporie. Cette « méthode » me permettra d'utiliser plusieurs concepts clés en devenir de la théorie littéraire contemporaine et des sciences humaines et sociales.

C'est à partir de certaines définitions des termes « antillanité », « politique » et « poétique » et de mon expérience de lecteur d'origine antillaise que je poserai mes questions à l'œuvre du poète-diplomate et à la critique de cette œuvre. Ma démarche générale visera, non pas à redresser des torts en blâmant l'auteur et/ou ses critiques, mais à établir un dialogue (acception de Gadamer) avec l'œuvre et sa critique. Ce faisant, je crois pouvoir démontrer la validité de mon hypothèse et apporter une contribution originale aux études persiennes.

### Inventaire et analyse
Inventaire et analyse des écrits consacrés au rapport SJP-Antilles; Recherches portant sur les origines sociales d'Alexis Leger, sa vie d'étudiant, de poète et de diplomate; Confronter les résultats de ces recherches avec la biographie de l'édition la Pléiade; Rassembler un corpus de correspondances pour une analyse « symptômale ».

### Étude des matériaux de la politique
Recherche et analyse des présupposés du politique : dialectique du privé/public, commandement/obéissance, ami/ennemi; Rôle du fonctionnaire d'État; Analyse de notions clés : « Étranger », « Europe » et « Européens », « Antilles » et « antillanité », « Amérique » et « Américains », « France » et « Français », …

## Étude des matériaux de la poétique

Lecture « symptômale » : composante de l'esthétique persienne; Relation entre l'esthétique et l'ontologie de l'être social; Rôle de la critique; Analyse de notions clés : « œuvre littéraire », « extranéité du poète », « noblesse de style », « témoignage littéraire » »; « Affiliation de SJP » (acception : E. Said); « Mythe littéraire » (acception : R. Étiemble); « Historicité de SJP » (acceptions : H.-G. Gadamer, H. Jauss et H. Meschonnic).

## Étude de la correspondance

Lecture « symptômale » du corpus (de lettres) retenu dans « Inventaire et Analyse »; Politique et esthétique de la lettre chez SJP; Rapport entre la correspondance, le mythe littéraire et la réception critique des poèmes; Idéologie de la correspondance et correspondance idéologique : SJP-V. Larbaud, SJP-P. Valéry, SJP-R. Caillois, SJP-A. MacLeish, SJP-D. Hammarskjold.

## Étude des poèmes

Lecture intertextuelle de poèmes de « Désir de Créole » à « Anabase ». But visé : souligner l'intertextualité des poèmes et cerner la relation politique-poétique-antillanité; Lecture intertextuelle de poèmes postérieurs à Anabase – but visé : suivre l'évolution de la relation.

5. BIBLIOGRAPHIE (détaillée, sinon exhaustive; au besoin, annexer des feuilles supplémentaires)

A. CORPUS (Œuvres d'Alexis Leger/Saint-John Perse)

## Remarques sur le corpus

C'est Leger, lui-même, qui a groupé dans un seul volume et sous le titre *Œuvres complètes*, une « biographie », sorte de résumé biographique écrit et annoté par l'auteur lui-même, une « œuvre poétique » comprenant dix poèmes, une « prose » qui rassemble des « discours », des « hommages » et « témoignages », et une « correspondance », sélection de lettres, missives officielles et fragments rapportés de conversations avec des traducteurs et critiques.

C'est cette édition parue en 1972 dans la Bibliothèque de la Pléiade et rééditée en 1982 qui me servira de jalon dans mes interrogations et recherches. Je dis bien « de jalon » car en se présentant, le poète n'a pas toujours respecté la chronologie de composition de ses œuvres et a procédé à certains groupements et modifications de poèmes qui pourraient induire le chercheur non averti en erreur. Il a aussi choisi de ne pas inclure dans ce volume un poème qui date de son enfance aux Antilles; le poème « Désir de Créole », écrit à la Guadeloupe et publié dans une revue coloniale, ne figure pas dans le volume de la Pléiade parce que, nous explique SJP, ce poème a été publié sans son autorisation.

Il convient aussi de souligner que la correspondance du volume de la Pléiade est une sélection de lettres et de communications à sens unique, sélection faite par l'auteur-éditeur lui-même. Ceci dit, vu la nature de mon étude (réception critique, mythe littéraire, historicité), il va de soi que je ne pourrai m'en tenir strictement au contenu et à la présentation du volume de la Pléiade. Il y donc tout

un travail de recherche et de documentation à effectuer.
Ce sera bien là d'ailleurs un des aspects originaux de mon
étude. Mon statut de membre de l'Association des Amis de
la Fondation Saint-John Perse me permettra d'avoir accès
à la bibliothèque personnelle de Leger et aux manuscrits
et textes déposés aux archives de la Fondation à Aix-en-
Provence.

Une bibliographie critique de neuf pages complétait ce
projet de recherche lors de son dépôt.

3

---

4   BIBLIOGRAPHIE (détaillée, sinon exhaustive; au besoin, annexer des feuilles supplémentaires)

A. CORPUS ( Oeuvres d'Alexis Leger/Saint-John Perse )

Remarques sur le corpus
        C'est Leger, lui-même, qui a groupé dans un seul volume et sous
le titre "Oeuvres complètes", une "biographie", sorte de résumé biographique écrit et annoté par l'auteur lui-même, une "oeuvre poétique"
comprenant dix poèmes, une "prose" qui rassemble des "discours", des
"hommages" et "témoignages", et une "correspondance", selection de
lettres, missives officielles et fragments rapportés de conversations
avec des traducteurs et critiques.
        C'est cette édition parue en 1972 dans la Bibliothèque de la
Pléiade et rééditée en 1982 qui me servira de jalon dans mes interrogations et recherches. Je dis bien -de jalon- car en se présentant, le
poète n'a pas toujours respecté la chronologie de composition de ses
oeuvres et a procédé à certains groupements et modifications de poèmes
qui pourraient induire le chercheur non averti en erreur. Il a aussi
choisi de ne pas inclure dans ce volume un poème qui date de son enfance
aux Antilles; le poème "Désir de Créole", écrit à la Guadeloupe et publié
dans une revue coloniale ne figure pas dans le volume de la Pléiade parce
que, nous explique le poète, ce poème a été publié sans son autorisation.
Il faut aussi souligner que la correspondance du volume de la Pléiade est
une sélection de lettres et de communications à sens unique, sélection
faite par l'auteur-éditeur lui-même. Ceci dit, et étant donné la nature
de mon étude ( réception critique, mythe littéraire, historicité ), il va
de soi que je ne pourrai m'en tenir strictement au contenu et à la présentation du volume de la Pléiade. Il y a donc tout un travail de recherche et de documentation à effectuer. Ce sera bien là d'ailleurs un des
aspects originaux de mon étude. Mon statut de membre de l'Association des
Amis de la Fondation Saint-John Perse me permettra d'avoir accès à la
bibliothèque personnelle de Leger et aux manuscrits et textes déposés aux
archives de la Fondation à Aix-en-Provence.

1. LES POÈMES ( Poèmes parus en revue, publiés en volume et en édition
                collective )
"Désir de Créole", La Guadeloupe littéraire, numéro 21, 15 mars, 1908.
"Des villes sur trois modes", Pan, numéro 4, juillet-aout 1908.

( Suite: voir BIBLIOGRAPHIE (Feuilles supplémentaires) )

---

Signature du candidat: _Gérard M. Hunt_    date _2/1 mai 1985_

---

FACULTÉ DES ÉTUDES SUPÉRIEURES

# LIST OF PUBLICATIONS
# CONSULTED AND/OR CITED

ANGENOT, Marc. *Les idéologies du ressentiment*, Montréal : XYZ éditeur, 1996.

ANGENOT, Marc. *La parole pamphlétaire : Typologie des discours modernes*, Paris : Payot, 1982.

ARNOLD, James A. ; RODRIGUEZ-LUIZ, Julio; DASH, J. Michael (Editors). *A History of Literature in the Caribbean, Volume 1: Hispanic and Francophone Regions*, Amsterdam/ Philadelphia: John Benjamins Publishing Company, 1994.

ARNOLD, James A. (Editor). *A History of literature in the Caribbean, Volume 2: English and Dutch –speaking regions*, Amsterdam/Philadelphia: John Benjamins Publishing Company, 2001.

ATTALI, Jacques. *Histoire du temps*, Paris : Fayard, coll. « Biblio Essais », 1992.

ATTALI, Jacques. *L'Homme nomade*, Librairie Arthème Fayard, 2003.

ATTALI, Jacques. *Une brève histoire de l'avenir*, Librairie Arthène Fayard, 2006.

BADEJO, Adekunle Fabian. *Salted Tongues – Modern Literature in St. Martin*, Sint Maarten: House of Nehesi, 2003.

BARREAU, Hervé. *Le Temps*, Paris : PUF, coll. « Que Sais-je? », 1996.

BINYON, Laurence. For the Fallen: The Times, September 21, 1914.

BLOOM, Harold. *Where Shall Wisdom Be Found?* New York: Riverhead Books, 2004.

BOSWELL, James. *Boswell's Life of Johnson*, London: 1904.

BURNET, John. *Early Greek Philosophy*, London: A & C Black (4th edition), 1930.

BUTE, Ruby. *Golden Voices of Smaatin*, Sint Maarten: House of Nehesi, 1989.

CÉSAIRE, Aimé. *Discours sur le colonialisme*. Éditions Présence Africaine, 1955.

CHAMOISEAU, Patrick. Méditations à Saint-John Perse in *La nouvelle anabase-Revue d'études persiennes* sous la direction de Loïc Céry, Numéro 1, Février 2006.

CHANLER, William Astor Jr. *And Did Those Feet in Ancient Time: A Seven Hundred Acre Island Reminiscence*, Outerbridge Books, Rockport, Maine, 1984.

CHRISTMAN, Robert A. Geology of St. Bartholomew, St. Martin, and Anguilla, Lesser Antilles, in *Bulletin of the Geological Society of America*, Vol. 64, pp.65-96,4PLS. January 1953.

CIORAN, Émil M. *Précis de décomposition*, Paris : Éditions Gallimard, 1949.

CIORAN, Émil M. *Syllogismes de l'amertume*, Paris : Éditions Gallimard, 1952.

DÉRRIDA, Jacques. *L'écriture et la différence*, Paris: Seuil, 1967.

DUBY, Georges. *Histoire de France. Des origines à nos jours* (Sous la direction de Georges Duby), Paris : Larousse, 1995.

FANON, Frantz. *Black Skin, White Masks*, New York: Grove Press, 1967.

FANON, Frantz. *The Wretched of the Earth*, New York: Grove Press, 1968.

FLOECK, Wilfried. Esthétique de la diversité. Pour une histoire du baroque littéraire en France in Papers on *French Seventeenth-Century Literature*, Paris-Seattle-Tubingen, 1989.

GIRARD, René. *La Violence et le Sacré*, Paris : Éditions Grasset, 1972.

GIRARD, René. *Le Bouc Émissaire*, Paris : Éditions Grasset, 1982.

GIRARD, René. *La route antique des hommes pervers*, Paris : Éditions Grasset, 1985.

GIRAUD, Fabien. (Preface) in *A Status for Saint-Martin-References of Hope - A collection of Studies on the Statutory Evolution of Saint-Martin*, Edited by Saint-Martin People's Consensus, House of Nehesi Publishers, St Martin, Caribbean, 2002.

GLASSCOCK, Jean. *Sint Maarten & Saint Martin. The Making of an Island*, Massachusetts: The Windsor Press Inc., 1985.

GLISSANT, Édouard. *Le discours antillais*, Paris : Éditions du Seuil, 1981.

GOSLINGA, Cornelis Ch. *A Short History of the Netherlands Antilles and Surinam*, The Hague: Martinus Nijhoff, 1979.

HARTOG, Johan. *History of Sint Maarten and Saint Martin*, Philipsburg: The Sint Maarten Jaycees, 1981.

HARTOG, François. *Le Miroir d'Hérodote: essai sur la représentation de l'autre*, Paris : Éditions Gallimard, 1980.

JEFFRY-PILOT, Daniella. *1963 A Landmark Year in St. Martin/1963-Année charnière à Saint-Martin*, Philipsburg, St. Martin, Caribbean, House of Nehesi Publishers, 2003.

JEFFRY, Daniella. *Le scandale statutaire sur l'île de Saint-Martin*, L'Harmattan, 2006.

JEFFRY, Daniella. *The Status Scandal on the Island of Saint-Martin*, Paris: L'Harmattan, 2006.

JOHNSON, Will. *Saban Lore. Tales from my Grandmother's Pipe*, 1979-1996.

JOHNSON, Will. *For the Love of St. Maarten*, 1987.

LAFLEUR, Gérard. *Les Caraïbes des Petites Antilles*, Paris : Éditions Karthala, 1992.

LAKE, Joseph Jr. *The Republic of St. Martin*, St. Martin, Caribbean: House of Nehesi Publishers, 2000.

LAKE, Joseph Jr. *Friendly Anger – The Rise of the Labor Movement in St. Martin*, St. Martin Caribbean, House of Nehesi Publishers, 2004.

LE GOFF, Jacques. *Histoire et mémoire*, Paris : Éditions Gallimard, 1988.

MATHEWS, Thomas G. The Spanish Domination of Saint Martin (1633-1648) in *Caribbean Studies*, Vol. 9, No.1, April 1969, University of Puerto-Rico: Institute of Caribbean Studies.

MONTAIGNE, Michel (Eyquem de). *Essays*, Translated with an introduction by J.M. Cohen, Penguin Books, 1958.

MOREAU, Jean-Pierre. *Un flibustier français dans la mer des Antilles 1618-1620*, Paris: Seghers, 1990.

MOREAU, Jean-Pierre. *Pirates – Flibuste et piraterie dans la Caraïbe et les mers du sud (1522-1727)*, Paris : Éditions Tallandier, 2006.

MONNIER, Yves. L'IMMUABLE ET LE CHANGEANT-*étude de la partie française de Saint-Martin, Collection Iles et Archipels, No 1 CRET Bordeaux III et CEGET (C.N.R.S.), 1983.*

NAIPAUL, V.S. *A House for Mr Biswas, London: Penguin Books, 1961.*

NAIPAUL, V.S. *The Middle Passage, London: Penguin Books, 1962.*

NAIPAUL, V.S. *The Mimic Men, London: Penguin Books, 1969.*

NAIPAUL, V.S. *A Writer's People - Ways of Looking and Feeling-An Essay in Five Poets, New York/Toronto: Alfred A. Knopf, 2008.*

PETITJEAN ROGET, Bernard. Pour comprendre la situation économique des Antilles in *Les Temps modernes* (39), avril-mai 1983, No 441-442, p.1853-1871.

PLACOLY, Vincent. *La vie et la mort de Marcel Gonstran*, Paris : Éditions Denoël, 1971.

POMIAN, Krzysztof. *L'Ordre du temps*, Paris : Éditions Gallimard, 1984.

POMIAN, Krzysztof. *Sur l'histoire*, Paris : Éditions Gallimard, 1999.

REVEL, Jean-François. *La grande parade – essai sur la survie de l'utopie socialiste*, Plon, 2000.

REVEL, Jean-François. *Histoire de la philosophie occidentale de Thalès à Kant*, Nil Éditions, 1994.

RICOEUR, Paul. *La mémoire, l'histoire, l'oubli*, Paris: Éditions du Seuil, 2000.

ROGER, Philippe. *L'ennemi américain. Généalogie de l'antiaméricanisme français*, Paris : Éditions du Seuil, 2002.

ROGER, Philippe. *The American Enemy – A History of French Anti-Americanism*, Translated by Sharon Bowman, Chicago: The University of Chicago Press, 2005.

ROGOZINSKI, Jan. *A Brief History of the Caribbean: From the Arawak and Carib to the Present.* (Revised Edition,) New York: Plume Penguin Group, 2000.

SAINT-JOHN PERSE. *Œuvres complètes*, Paris : Éditions Gallimard, 1972.

SAINT-JOHN PERSE. *Œuvres complètes*, Paris : Éditions Gallimard, 1982.

SAINT-MARTIN : OBJECTIF STATUT - Repères pour l'espoir : Recueil d'études sur l'évolution statutaire de Saint-

Martin, Edité par Consensus Populaire Saint-Martinois, House of Nehesi Publishers, St Martin, Caribbean, 2002.

ST-MARTIN'S GAZETTE – La gazette historique de St-Martin (English and French text) Réalisé par W.I. PUB, correspondant à St. Maarten : Ph.Tisseaux, Grand-Case , Saint-Martin, Printed in the U.S.A. Hallmark Press, Miami (Undated)

SEKOU, Lasana M. *Born Here*, Sint Maarten: House of Nehesi, 1986.

SEKOU, Lasana M. (Editor) *National Symbols of St. Martin – A Primer*, Philipsburg: House of Nehesi Publishers, 1997.

SÉVILLIA, Jean. *Historiquement correct. Pour en finir avec le passé unique*, Perrin, Paris, 2003.

TODOROV, Tzvetan. *Nous et les autres*, coll. « Points-Seuil », 1989.

TODOROV, Tzvetan. *La conquête de l'Amérique – La question de l'autre*, Éditions du Seuil, 1982.

WILLIAMS, Eric. *From Columbus to Castro: The History of the Caribbean 1492-1969*, New York and Evanston: Harper & Row, Publishers, 1970.

WILLIAMS, Eric. *Inward Hunger The Education of a Prime Minister*, Chicago: The University of Chicago Press, 1971.